Send the gunboats up the Mersey

Brian Benjamin

DEDICATION

Dedicated to those who fought for the rights and the NHS that we take for granted today.

CONTENTS

ACKNOWLEDGMENTS

A huge thanks to the invaluable service of Liverpool's record library at Central library.

Also thanks to my Dad who if he had not told me as a kid that Churchill sent a gunboat up the Mersey, would have known nothing about a major part of Liverpool's history.   I think my Nana Benji might have been referring to the 1919 riots , but without being told the story I never would have found out about the transport strike, bloody Sunday, and the first gunboats sent up to the Mersey.

INTRODUCTION

There are periods of history that slowly fade away like autumn leaves as the years go by despite the importance of events. Stories still linger on that gain mythical status that sometimes it is hard to distinguish from what is true and what isn't.

Working class history is something that is scarcely discussed and the influence that ordinary people have had on history. In terms of history at school it's pretty much topics regarding monarchs or the build-up to the first world war and then the second. Nothing is taught about the aftermath after the wars and how after the second world war the positive impact of the NHS and the welfare state had on the population. Nor is there much taught about the abject poverty and the fight that working class people had to endure to get better working conditions and pay. Even though those earlier fights have led to better working rights today. Nothing also has been mentioned about the violence that was meted out on striking workers by Police and soldiers.

Some of this has been addressed by the movie Peterloo which has quite rightly received a lot of publicity when the movie was released last year. It showed the brutality of the local militia with the cavalry charging a crowd of protestors in Manchester who were campaigning for political reform. Fifteen people were killed with over four hundred people injured. As the battle of Waterloo had taken place four years earlier the aftermath was named Peterloo to enforce the impact of charging a peaceful crowd.

Articles praised the movie and spoke about how much more should be written about working class history and the injustices they fought against. Despite this, scarcely much has been written about events that have helped shaped our history and brought about more equality in terms of working rights.

The period that the gunboats were sent up the Mersey during the 1911 transport strike was termed as the 'great unrest.' Yet despite the biggest city outside of London at the time being brought to a standstill and two gunboats being sent up the Mersey, nothing is mentioned. It took a lot of research and even then, dead ends to try and establish what was true and what wasn't.

According to most history books the 'great unrest,' was just a minor bump in the history of time. Nothing significant, until August 1914 when Britain entered the war following Germany's invasion of Belgium.

Yet the great unrest and the 1911 transport strike is a period that deserves to be aired. In many ways it has more significance for our history in the sense that it is only a hundred years ago and in the grander scheme of things was the first step to bringing about not just fair wages and conditions but to better housing, welfare, and a health system that we all rely on.

Just like Peterloo, violence was used by the authorities during the 1911 transport strike when thousands attended a meeting outside of St. George's Hall to listen to one of the prominent Trade Unionists Tom Mann. The aftermath led to a riot and two deaths with Churchill infamously sending two gunboats up the Mersey with the guns pointing at the city itself. It was in many respects a general strike, such was the economic importance of Liverpool at the time but scarcely mentioned today.

This book aims to address this by giving not just an account of what happened in 1911 but the background towards it. Despite being a rich city, surrounded by beautiful buildings, poverty was rife with working life incredibly hard that people were treated no better than chattel. It is also an explanation as to the core reasons behind the events of the transport strike as well as trying to give a picture of what Liverpool was like during that period.

Initially the book was solely meant to be about the 1911 transport strike, but I didn't want to stretch the events purely for the sake of a word count. Added to which it would lose the momentum of what happened and put the reader off. Instead I stuck to the story which I have hopefully made as informative as possible.

However, I have also added some other articles about events that have scarcely been mentioned and airbrushed out of history. The end of the first world war was a place of uncertainty and Britain was no different to other countries that had seen Kings and rulers being overthrown. 1919 was a year of mutinies in the army, strikes, and riots that it is quietly dubbed as 'the year of near revolution.'

In that year there were plans by Churchill to end the Bolshevik threat by wanting to invade Russia. This despite the country having just come out of a long and bloody four-year war. Most conscripts wanted to be demobbed and try to return to normal life. Not surprisingly, when this seemed to be under threat mutinies broke out with soldiers against soldiers at one point as the authorities tried to regain order.

During 1919 troops and tanks were dispatched to cities such as London, Glasgow, and Liverpool with yet another gunboat being sent up the Mersey. There was another Police charge in Glasgow that resulted in injuries and a riot with the authorities getting twitchy that there was a Bolshevik uprising on the cards especially when red flags were being flown in Glasgow.

Yet despite all this not much is known about these events. Whilst researching this book I read Roy Hattersley's biography about Lloyd George. Considering the seriousness of the events mentioned there was no mention of the 1911 transport strike and one very small paragraph about the events in 1919. For anyone without some background you would think it was a minor dispute rather than one that sent panic within the Government who at one point feared revolution.

Although the above events seem not to be linked, they were in some respects what led to a Labour landslide during the 1945 election. As a result, and Labour's aim of building for the future it led to the formation of the welfare state and the NHS. Something that is a significant part of our history such was the impact of Nye Bevan's policies. Despite this I don't recall ever being taught about post-war Britain and why Labour won such a massive mandate in 1945.

I have also wrote about the 'race riots,' in Liverpool an event that as awful as it was needs to be remembered because as the philosopher George Santayana said 'those that do not remember the past, are condemned to repeat it.'

Due to the book being about events in history that is scarcely mentioned there are also articles on Dixie Dean, football's first number nine which I first wrote For these football times website. In his time, Dean was the footballing equivalent of the baseball star Babe Ruth. A talented footballer who scored a record sixty-nine goals in a season that saw Everton win the 1932-33 league title.

Researching Dean's life was akin to something from a movie. From making a comeback from a motorcycle crash where he was told he wouldn't walk never mind play, to opposing Nazis, and being a world class footballer who deserves to be up there with the big names of Best, Pele, Maradona, and Messi.

Also included is an article about Joe Fagan that was also featured in these football times website. Winning a treble of league championship, European cup, and league cup in your first season should be enough for you to earn your place of the managerial greats, yet Joe Fagan is scarcely known outside of Liverpool.

It isn't just about the two seasons that Joe Fagan was in charge but being influential within the bootroom. Like Bill Shankly and Bob Paisley, Joe Fagan was just as important in not just dragging Liverpool out of the second division but turning them into a 'bastion of invincibility.'

Admittedly, I have bulked the book with some football articles that I have had published. So, if you like history and football you'll be made up. Even if your not the story about Dixie Dean and Socrates is definitely worth a read with the former being something out of a movie.

Hopefully there will be something out there for everyone within this book and although it is a self-published one I hope that it gives the opportunity of at least trying to keep the light of working class history alive, especially as it had an impact on our lives today.

Brian Benjamin.

THE MAKING OF LIVERPOOL

The city itself grew from being a small fishing town in Lancashire to being one of the biggest in the world. As a result, the population grew and gives an idea of what it was like living and working in Liverpool and the seeds that would lead to the transport strike of 1911 and gunboats being sent up the Mersey.

With trade growing in the new world of America and the West Indies so too did Liverpool's port due to the logistics of where it was located. The slave trade is one of the nefarious periods in the city's history but Liverpool' economy started to grow because of it. Whether it was through handling slaves through the ports or trading with cotton via the plantations it was how Liverpool began to make its wealth. Indeed, Liverpool formed one corner of the slave triangle and it is estimated in 1807 that three quarters of slave ships set sail from the port of Liverpool.

Although slavery was abolished in the UK in 1833 the city was still indirectly involved through its trading with the USA. During the American civil war of 1861-65, Liverpool heavily supported the Confederates with CSS Alabama being built at Birkenhead. The historian Sven Beckert stated that Liverpool 'was the most pro-Confederate place in the world outside the Confederacy itself.'

The economy still thrived even after slavery was abolished in the States as the British Empire was at its most influential. Again, it was the city's ideal position of its ports and trading centres that the city came second only to London in terms of wealth and population. Back in Liverpool's golden period it was like New York in terms of a growing metropolis whose growth came through its docks and immigration.

As the industrial revolution exploded more and more people from the rural areas of England, Wales, and Ireland went to seek work in cities like Liverpool. Due to the proximity of North Wales and regular ships sailing from Ireland to Liverpool it became a popular destination for those hoping to start a new life. Between 1801 and 1851 Liverpool's population grew from 78,000 to 376,000. By 1911 the population had doubled to more than 746,000. Many were Irish immigrants due to the famine who had fled to Liverpool in the hope of gaining passage to the new world of America or stayed in Liverpool. Between 1841 and 1851 the population of Irish born residents residing in Liverpool rose from 17.3 percent to 22.3 percent. Even in 1891 it was still 12.6 percent which was about ten times the proportion of Irish born people living in other parts England and Wales.

Not that Liverpool's immigration growth solely relied on Ireland. There were large communities of Italian, Scandinavian, Spanish, Portuguese, Chinese, West Indies, and Jamaican to name but a few. It was very much a metropolitan city with a bustling hotpot of various cultures that brought vibrancy, culture, and life to Liverpool. Even the city's known cuisine Scouse is a version of Lobscouse which was a stew that came from sailors from Northern Europe like Germany and the countries from Scandinavia.

This was something that appealed to Charles Dickens who that he visited Liverpool regularly. In turn he was also popular as Charles Dickens gave many public readings of his works most notably at St. George's hall. Such was his love of the city that after performing a reading in Manchester, Dickens promptly travelled to Liverpool to stay overnight.

George Dolby who was a close friend and manager of Charles Dickens said 'it is not to be wondered at that Mr Dickens should prefer to return to this his favourite hotel, and, except London, his favourite city.' Dickens himself even referred to Liverpool 'as that rich and beautiful port.'

Liverpool was a city that Charles Dickens like to explore. Like most of his works he was keen to visit and highlight the deprivation and poverty that he witnessed. It was also a case as it is for most writers to also see characters and provide a rough guide to ideas for stories. Liverpool was metropolitan, vibrant city that like London was a mixture of architecture grandeur, high wealth with poverty and hardship entwined.

Dickens wrote about his experience when he enlisted as a special constable, patrolling the docks of Liverpool.

The talk of 'a strange world,' by Dickens is as though he has lifted up the tattered mat to show another world that existed amongst the riches in Liverpool. Certainly there is a sense that danger lurks by as he talks of unsuspected sailors being stalked by men and women, looking to rob or swindle their prey of money, but Dickens finds a light hearted moment when he stumbles upon a ale house.

A Spanish Youth is delicately playing a guitar whilst Dickens also mentions about a 'young girl of delicate prettiness of face, figure, and dress,' playing a 'kind of piano accordion.'

There was British Jack, a little maudlin and sleepy, lolling over his empty glass…there was Loafing Jack of the Stars and Stripes…there was Spanish Jack, with curls of black hair, rings in his ears, and a knife not far from his hand…there were Maltese Jack, and Jack of Sweden, and Jack the Finn.'

As trade grew so too did the city of Liverpool's wealth. The buildings that we see today from Water Street, the Pier Head, St. George's Hall, the Walker art gallery and the museums are the legacy left today from that era. Indeed, the Walker art gallery housed a collection of valuable work outside of London. Liverpool also saw itself at the forefront of medicine with the School of tropical medicine.

A house through time that was shown on BBC2 that featured on 62 Faulkner Street in Liverpool highlighted the wealth that some of the inhabitants had. When it was first built it was a highly sought, fashionable part of Liverpool that wasn't cheap to buy. With its Georgian architecture the only other properties similar are based in London and Bristol. There is of course Huskisson street, Rodney street amongst a few that it is now known as the Georgian quarter.

It wasn't just around this area that housed the rich elite. Just jump a bus towards Princes Park and you will see large fashionable houses (with the majority now converted into apartments) that only the rich could afford.

As you go towards the end of Princes Park that heads towards Smithdown road you can notice the markings of a gate that only allowed the inhabitants of the area in. Unless you were a servant or a trades person then you would not be permitted to enter.

Sefton, Stanley, and Calderstones park to name a few also show the money that was spent in ensuring there was something beautiful to stroll through. Look at the palm house and the features that are in the park and this is all due to big money that enabled the parks to happen.

Despite the now found riches that trade brought to the city it was mainly the merchants, bankers, and local businessmen who profited. Liverpool was a city that saw the haves and the have nots brushing side by side on the streets, but they were a solar system apart from the lives that they led.

Work was mainly found either on the ships, docks or domestic servitude in one of the big houses. Having a servant was a sign of respectability with those on the lower middle-class ladder having a maid who would be the 'maid of all work.' Some servants would be 'rescued,' from orphanages to help with demand. However, with factories and shops allowing evenings off and the odd weekend it wasn't surprising that not many people were keen on domestic servitude. Nevertheless, it was a major source of occupation for those needing to live. In 1911 there were 1.27 million indoor domestic servants.

Life for those working on the docks or other menial work would find themselves living in slum housing. Due to money being scarce families would be forced to rent a small dilapidated room. It would look grim with damp, lack of sanitation, and clean water which would lead to illness due to the overcrowding of these crumbling buildings. Even from viewing from the outside they would look like rotten teeth as the tenements and houses were stacked closely to each other.

Liverpool in that era was certainly a tale of two cities in one. Rich, big buildings that flaunted the cities wealth might have impressed those visiting Liverpool like William Defoe or Charles Dickens but there was another world around the corner. One of want and deprivation who were living way below the bread line.

The Reverend Richard Acland Armstrong a resident of Liverpool in the late 1890's wrote 'I had seen wealth. I had seen poverty. But never before had I seen the two so jammed together. Never before had I seen streets, loaded with all that wealth can buy, lined with the hopeless penury.'

Due to the high rise of diseases and typhoid fever that engulfed the city, Liverpool became the first city to appoint a Medical Officer of Health the celebrated Doctor William Duncan in which a self-titled pub in Queens Square is named after him. The Council though, only voted to appoint him part-time rather than full time.

It was through Doctor Duncan that moves were made to improve sanitation, cleaner water to eradicate cholera and typhoid fever. Yet his successor sixty years later Doctor Hope advised the Council 'there was not a city in this country, nay in Europe, which could produce anything like the squalor that his officials found in some of Liverpool's backstreets.'

For some such as the lower middle-class they were precariously close to finding themselves on the bread line. All it took would be a serious illness or the loss of a job. Poverty like disease could quickly tap you on the shoulder and knock you spiralling into a life of squalor.

Working at the docks

Just as the ships and docks were the heartbeat of Liverpool's new-found wealth it became the main source of employment. Certainly, with a large population it meant that wages and rights were severely restricted due to demand for work. Despite the grandiose Victorian morality and religious piety, it did not stop the idea of making a profit above all else.

Working at the docks was long, hard, and tough. It wasn't well paid, the conditions were poor, and there was no guarantee of regular work due to the casualisation of dock workers. Each morning under the 'tally system,' you had to wait to see if you would be picked to work or be left doing nothing and without pay. Due to the erratic nature of the system you could quite easily find yourself in financial difficulties.

Surprisingly though, Brian Towers in the splendid book 'Waterfront Blues,' writes that the fight against casualisation came from the Unions own members. The belief being that they had more choice when they could work rather than the promise of regular work.

Liverpool's waterfront saw a vast array of work from working in the warehouses, dock gatemen, painters, carpenters, carters who were employed by carter firms. There were crews for the tugboats that hummed up and down the Mersey. Firemen, grease monkeys, sailors and even work on passenger ships as stewards, cooks, and other staff to keep the ship running were also viable employment alternatives.

Employees rights were way low on the employer's agenda who were more interested in profits. As far they were concerned it was their money and expertise that was being risked with the worker receiving the benefit of their entrepreneurship.

Not surprisingly this was viewed differently by the workers who felt that the vast profits were made on the back of their labour.

As people are want to do when being treated unfairly they looked at ways at fighting back. It wasn't just about better wages but hours and conditions. Even health and safety issues were the employees were at risk could result in anger especially if someone got badly injured or even killed.

Even though there were dangers in loading and unloading of cargo there were numerous incidents of corners being cut in order to get the job done on time and without having to pay extra for the correct equipment. A serious injury could see you incapacitated were you wouldn't be able to work and provide food on the table. In some cases, the dreaded workhouse could beckon if you couldn't keep your head above water.

Being killed at work would have major repercussions for the family who would have to try and find some other ways of bringing money in.

Fed up at being treated like chattel, men would discuss and meet up to discuss what they should do. Withdrawing your labour was the biggest weapon that the employee had. It did lead to wildcat strikes over conditions and pay but the biggest chance of success was being organised and belonging to a Trade Union.

The employer though heavily frowned at the idea of their employees joining a Trade Union. Consulting with trade union shop stewards was something considered beneath them and would lead to a hit in their pockets. An organised trade union could pose problems which could see a strike if the men had grievances.

Joining or trying to form a trade union was heavily frowned and discouraged. Anyone causing problems of this nature would be shown the door and would find it hard to find work at the docks. Even joining a union could see you being viewed as a dangerous agitator and being dismissed. For the employer it was best to nip these matters in the bud and to make an example, as to them it could lead to further trouble.

It was not surprising that there were some flashpoints when the dockers called wildcat strikes over conditions and wages. At various points these were resolved but there was a tension building up between the workers and employers. This wasn't just in Liverpool but right across the country. Whether that was miners, ship builders, mills, factories, and steel workers who felt that deserved to be treated and paid fairly.

Anger and disgust about poverty was also rising especially when children went without food and decent clothing. Disease was rife and a low life expectancy for those unlucky to be born or to fall into poverty.

Politics was coming to the fore during this era as trade unionists and those wanting a better life for their children realised that the only way to change things, was through activism. It led to the formation of the Labour party in 1900 and during the period of the transport strike was still very much in its infancy.

The British Empire may still have been at its height with huge amounts of trade and money certainly going through Liverpool with the rich inhabitants were quite happy to show their wealth or be philanthropists to favoured charities in order to gain favour when they met their maker.

Nevertheless, there was a change in the wind that was blowing. For the employer they might have been happy with the status-quo, but their employees were getting dissatisfied with their treatment and poor quality of life. It was for no better word the beginning of the fight back. 1911 is quietly termed as 'the great unrest,' with the events of the miners in Tonypandy in 1910 being noted the country and certainly Liverpool was building up to their own industrial unrest. Like every major event it had been bubbling underneath like a pot on the cooker, but it wasn't far off from blowing the lid off and frightening the elite.

Despite the mumblings and complaints, the beginning of 1911 was pretty much like it was in years gone by. Family, work, and trying to live life as best as you could. Certainly, there would be discussions about what was happening in the day and what was going on in work.

There would be other escapes on whether it was the ale house, cinema, music halls or football. Liverpool was becoming a city were sport flourished and like many other cities and towns across the country none more so than football. As befitting a big city, they too had two big clubs in Liverpool and Everton who averaged attendances over 18,000 for the 1910-11 season.

Nevertheless, the spark would be ignited later that year with one event building a domino effect and lead not just to a transport strike but an unofficial general strike within the city of Liverpool.

THE BEGINNING OF THE TRANSPORT STRIKE

Skirmishes between the employers and workers was nothing new. For the former it was about keeping things as cheap as possible and controlling the workforce whilst the latter wanted better wages and conditions. Also, there was an increase for trade union recognition to ensure that their deal would not be renegaded and that any changes had to go through their elected officials.

For many the seamen's strike' was the spark that set off the train of events that saw a Liverpool general strike which in turn led to violence and Churchill agreeing to send two gunboats up the Mersey.

The start of the seamen's dispute was the sailors wanting an end to the humiliating medical inspections demanded by the ship owners. They also asked for their wages to be paid when the ship was in port and not be held until they returned home. A demand for better conditions on the ships was also put forward as well as an increase in wages by ten shillings to bring the seamen's wages up to £5 10s per month, as well as trade union recognition.

Syndicalism was becoming popular in the trade union and movement with the idea of workers supporting each other. It meant that there was a lot of cross worker support which led to the transport workers federation who represented seamen, dockers, carters joining the Industrial Syndicalist Education League, who had elected Tom Mann a prominent speaker as their leader.

Due to this alliance a meeting was called and to be held at St. George's Hall plateau on the 31st May 1911. Thousands attended to listen to speeches from trade union officials such as Havelock Wilson, Joseph Cotter, Will Thorne MP, and James Sexton.

It was quite a passionate affair as they spoke about being treated and paid fairly. How they had to stand up for themselves. Crucially though they appealed to other workers such as the dockers to come out and support the seamen. Strength was in solidarity and numbers in order to bring the employer to the table and reach an agreement.

There was hostility from the employers who feared at what the concessions could lead to. Again, profit was at their foremost thoughts as well as the thought of having to discuss changes or make safety concessions with the trade unions.

However, the workers were not letting up this time. If anything, it was being stepped up as on the 14th June 1911 five hundred firemen refused to sign on to man the liners with the Baltic being one of the ships.

Upon realising that the seamen's union held the winning cards and that if this dispute continued any longer it would affect their profits the employer looked to trying to reach an agreement. Unfortunately, from the shipping owners' perspective they made a grave error by deciding that the best course of action was to allow the shipping companies to make individual settlements. Their reasoning for this was that the companies could decide what deal was acceptable from their side.

What the shipping owners should have done was show a collective front when negotiating with the union. Instead it saw seamen across the country negotiating with members of the shipping federation. Not that the latter was averse to using dirty tactics in forcing the strikers back to work. They would run some ships whilst laying off others with the intent of forcing the seamen back to work. However, as the strike was strongly supported it did not have any success and deals had to be struck.

In Liverpool the shipping owners (who were not members of the shipping federation) decided that the best course of action was to negotiate with the seamen's union via a committee led by Alfred Booth, who was also the nephew of Charles Booth the well-known reformer.

Negotiations were ironically easier with the larger companies as a deal was met with the Seamen's union. The biggest problem came with the smaller ship owners who were intent on keeping wages at the old levels. They cited that they couldn't afford the increase due to business constraints.

Upon seeing how the strike was costing not just the ship owners but various other businesses related to the ports, pressure came from the board of trade to sort out an agreement promptly. Reluctantly they agreed and so it seemed that a potential trade disaster for Liverpool had been averted.

There was a general smugness and self-congratulatory pats on the back with the local Liverpool paper the Daily Courier heaping praise on 'their generosity towards the seamen.' For them it was a return to normality and making profits.

However, amongst their vanity they had not counted on four thousand dockers walking out the following morning with some probably choking on their breakfast when they heard the news. No doubt there was those that felt making concessions would have a domino effect with other workers who plied their trade

As it was the dockers went out for trade union recognition for the national union of dock labourers (NUDL), better working conditions, and wages.

Whilst they tried to recover from this new blow, they then received further news that the entire crew of the Canadian Pacific Empress came out in support of the dockers. Not only did they come out but encouraged other seamen from other ships on the Atlantic run to join them. All it took was for them to walk down the port and appealing to their fellow seamen sense of camaraderie.

The chats would have consisted of the support that the dockers had given them and about standing together. Friends would have encouraged others and the mood was resolute and determined that they had to support the dockers.

By the end of the day the entire dock, sea, and land trades, brought the Liverpool docks to a halt such was the support for the dockers. The biggest shock and worry for the ship owners and other employers were the spontaneity of support. What would have frightened them more was the altruistic view of the seamen and other workers that came out to support the dockers, especially as they had nothing to gain.

This view was summed in a quote for one of the local papers as a ship steward from the Empress Britain was quoted about why they had gone out when they got the concessions that they had asked for in the seamen strike had been agreed. 'Yes, I admit we got what we wanted... we have no grievance with the company, but there is a question of honour at stake. The dock labourers struck purely in sympathy with us, and now we are going to do the same for them.'

For these ship owners, employers, government and the establishment it would have sent a cold shiver down their necks. In their world there was a hierarchy which people were expected to follow. Whether the order was from an aristocrat, officer, sergeant, foreman, Union shop stewards, the position was to be respected. It was this perceived lack of regard for the natural order of things that baffled the shipping owners and government officials who would have worried where this could lead to.

Even the trade union officials were taken by surprise as it was initially led by their members and other workers rather than being union driven. Like anything else where politics was involved there was probably a few noses knocked out of joint that it was not them initially leading from the front. Added to which some officials would have felt that they too might lose control and indirectly believed in a hierarchy.

To stop this escalating even further and to try to knock the wind out of the strikers sails, the employer looked to meet with the strike committee as soon as possible. The docks after all were the artery of Liverpool's economy and this dispute needed to be resolved as quickly as possible.

One of the first agreements was recognition of the NUDL with some concessions to the rules on wages and conditions. However, the employer wanted to break up the momentum and certainly did not want to concede to all the demands readily. So, it was that the employer wanted to agree to a conference with the strike committee regarding further pay and conditions which had been put on the table. It was hoped that by stalling for time the support for the dock workers would die down as the excitement and support from the seamen would evaporate. This in theory would give them a stronger hand when negotiating.

Although the conference was agreed by the strike committee with the recommendation to members to return to work pending the outcome of the conference there were those who were not happy with the agreement. The main disagreement came from the North End members of the NUDL who refused to return to work on the back of this compromise.

It may well have been the case that the NUDL North End members saw through the dock employers' ruse of buying time and wanted something more concrete than words. Nevertheless, a return to work was finally achieved by the 3rd July 1911 as the likes of Tom Mann, James Sexton, Joseph Cotter and other NUDL officials persuaded the North End members to agree with their strategy of the conference.

Due to the recent successes of the walkout the NUDL saw a massive increase in their membership. Indeed, there was a huge surge of workers joining trade unions right throughout the city. No doubt to the chagrin of the ship owners and other employers there was an outbreak of strikes varying from cotton porters, tug boat workers, and women shoemakers at the Walton rubber factories. All of whom wanted better pay and conditions.

Industrial discontent was crackling like a hot fire as the tramway workers joined the National Union of Enginemen, Firemen, Mechanical, and Electrical workers. They too would also be going out on strike along with the railway workers.

The railway strike lights the fuse of revolt.

1911 was to see a particular hot summer with another dispute this time more national rather than local with the railway workers. Ironically the dockers and shipowners were reaching an agreement when the dispute would take another twist that would plunge the city into uncertainty and revolt.

Lloyd George was a wily old politician as he attempted to stave off anything firm with regards to the railway workers demands. Despite the government setting up conciliation boards to deliver progress on pay, hours, and conditions they were still far away from agreeing to a deal.

There was also frustration at their own officials in putting pressure on the bosses and strategy in resolving their grievances. This was especially true of James Sexton who the railway workers felt was not pulling his finger out quickly enough.

It was in Liverpool that an unofficial strike began at the North dock's depot of the Lancashire and Yorkshire railway on the 5th August. This was to lead to a chain of events that would see a general strike in Liverpool. A dispute so serious due to the economic importance of the docks, that it caused panic amongst the government.

No doubt after feeling that the previous disputes were dealt with leniently the railway bosses decided that it needed a different tact to show the strikers that they meant business and what the repercussions would be over their actions. The strikers were promptly blacklisted, and replacements were brought in. If they hoped that this would cow the railway strikers' then they were sorely mistaken. The bosses might as well have kicked a beehive and not expect to be stung in response.

A domino effect hit Liverpool as the dock workers, tram workers, seamen, and anyone such as carters who transported goods to the docks went out in support of the railway workers. Predictably the official rail union leaders were late in giving their support and making a national strike an official one and were forced into it by their striking members.

Even though the NUDL had signed an agreement regarding the terms and conditions with the bosses of the docks a week earlier, they took unkindly to the dockers support of the railway strike. In response they announced a lockout from the 14th August citing that the dockers were in breach of contract for refusing to unload goods transported by rail. This in effect now brought the docks to a standstill with nothing moving in or out.

As a result of this and no doubt causing more anxiety for the bosses and authorities a strike committee was formed. This was to ensure that there was some organisation and planning to make certain that the strike was effective. It also made the authorities fully aware that they were serious and not to be trifled with.

The only goods that could leave the docks was essential items such as milk and grain. However, some of the companies had tried to take advantage of this gesture as they attempted to bring items such as beer through. When it was discovered what the actual items were, there was uproar from the strikers who overturned the vehicle with the barrels taken by the crowd.

With the dispute growing stronger there was no doubt that the strike committee now unofficially ran Liverpool, as all of the city's main trade was came through the docks. Not only was it important to Liverpool but also essential for the country economically. Consequently, the longer the strike went on the more damage it would cause in terms of trade.

It also didn't help the government's nerves were frayed as industrial disputes were breaking out across the country. The authorities were becoming increasingly alarmed at the general unrest and where it could lead to if it continued to burn furiously. There had been Tonypandy a year before and in August there was the Llanelli riots when two strikers were shot dead by the Worcestershire regiment.

No doubt panic was also setting in as the authorities in Liverpool wanted to reassert control by requesting extra Policing. The increase of the crowds on the picket lines and more workers such as the goods porters going out on strike meant that the authorities felt more man power was required to keep order.

Winston Churchill who was the Home Secretary at the time was a man not shy in showing and using force as the miners in Tonypandy discovered in 1910. To ensure extra security and to take back control he not only sent in the extra Policing who arrived by Leeds and Birmingham, but troops and cavalry. By the 12th August it was estimated that there were 5,000 troops and 24,000 Police ready to be used by the authorities if needed.

It was now leading to a standoff between the authorities and the strikers. The mood from reading accounts at the time was one of apprehension at seeing the extra Police and troops. Although it didn't stop some from booing and hurling insults when the Police arrived from Leeds and Birmingham.

Whether the authorities intended it or not there was now a siege mentality engulfing the city. Rather than be intimidated the strikers were defiant and angry at being treated as the enemy. This mood crackled like lightening when it was discovered that the troops brought into the city had also been provided with live ammunition.

Although a bullet had not been fired the feeling by those living in the city was that they were on the brink of civil war. Either way it had become a dangerous game of bluff by the authorities. With the introduction of Police, army reinforcements, and later two gunboats moored in the Mersey it was a case of whether they would show their hand and suffer the repercussions as a result.

Equally for the strike committee it would have given them much food for thought. This after all was an industrial dispute for better rights, wages, and union recognition. What they didn't want was a physical fight were people would be hurt simply for fighting for their rights. However, to back down at this point would see any ground lost that had previously been made and losing the current initiative. So, it was that they continued the strike but equally determined not to give the authorities any excuse to use force.

To show the full strength of support of the strike a meeting was scheduled for Sunday 13th August at St. George's plateau. There was to be an array of popular speakers such as the prominent Syndicalist and trade unionist Tom Mann, who had many successes under his belt such as the 1888 London dock strike. Mann was a skilled orator who could connect and raise morale with a crowd. Listening to Tom Mann made you believe that anything was possible, and that right was on your side.

Upon hearing this the authorities stepped up the use of Police and troops around the city to ensure that they would not be caught out if it led to trouble.

Not that there was any indication of that, but such was the paranoia, no chances were taken.

BLOODY SUNDAY AND GUNBOATS UP THE MERSEY

Despite the strong presence of the Police and soldiers, nothing was moving in or out without the strike committees' say so. The mood amongst people was buoyant and defiant at the companies and authorities using the full weight of the government against them.

For the ordinary person they could only take so much of living in poverty, being exploited and treated as a commodity and not a human being. This was the start of being paid a fair wage, of decent conditions, and recognising trade unions so that when the dispute was over, they had some protection against the companies if they attempted to retract their promises. Added to which they could continue the fight for a better workplace and employment rights.

The summer of 1911 was a particularly good and hot one according to the accounts of that year. As the seconds of the clock eventually counted down to the Sunday of the strike meeting, crowds of people slowly marched towards St. George's Hall with the mood being warm and upbeat like the weather. Reading the accounts there was a general good feeling amongst the people. This was their moment for their voice to be heard and to show solidarity amongst each other.

A mass of people from the North and South end of Liverpool all made their way towards the city centre to St. George's Hall. Banners were held aloft with loud chatter and laughs as they made their way up the roads to the plateau itself.

Liverpool at that time was rife with sectarianism with much distrust between the Catholic and Protestant communities. So, it must have made the authorities turn pale when they saw the two groups marching proudly together. An account of Fred Bowers an eyewitness at the time gave his account of workers marching from all over Liverpool proudly said 'From Orange Garston, Everton and Toxteth Park, from Roman Catholic Bootle and the Scotland Road area they came. Forgotten were their religious feuds. The Garston band had walked five miles and their drum major proudly whirled his sceptre twined with orange and green ribbon.'

'Never in the history of this or any other country had the majority and might of the humble toiler been so displayed. A wonderful spirit of humour and friendliness permeated the atmosphere.'

More and more people were marching up that it must have seemed as if most of Liverpool had made their way up towards the city centre. It was estimated that 80,000 people attended the plateau at St. George's Hall. The photographs that were taken of that day certainly do not exaggerate that estimation. With trade union banners proudly held aloft, people shimmying up lamp posts and any other vantage point that it resembled the Arab spring of 2010. It would probably be fair to say that the last time the city had seen such a huge crowd was in 2005 when Liverpool FC brought back the European cup.

For the people attending, this was a proud and historic occasion. Looking at the pictures you can't help but be uplifted by the smiles and just simply the huge tide of support that the people had for each other. They were just ordinary people with their own families and friends. They had their hopes, dreams, and talents just like anyone of today. Their fight was for a better future and to be treated fairly. As the old saying goes, you can only push people so far, before they hit back. Now was this moment.

Despite the mood of defiance there were no accounts of plans to cause trouble. This was to be a demonstration to give themselves a voice and show the support that the strikers had. Indeed, Tom Mann had reached an agreement with the Head Constable that demo could go ahead. A further agreement was made that the presence of the Police and military would be kept to a minimum to avoid any confrontation. The strike committee had called on 'all workers taking part in the demonstration to conduct themselves with manly dignity.'

By all accounts the mood was relaxed and good nature with the crowds enjoying the sun as they waited to hear Tom Mann speak Fred Bowers in his book 'rolling stonemason,' speaks of 'women and children were ranked tier upon tier of them and the meeting was perfectly orderly.'

A huge cheer and applause broke out as Tom Mann addressed the crowd from one of the five lorries placed among the crowd defiantly cried 'we cannot, in the face of the military and extra police drafted into the city, have effectual picketing and we cannot but accept the display of force as a challenge. We shall be prepared to declare on Tuesday morning a general strike, that will mean a strike of all transport men of all classes.'

Mann went on to prophetically warn the crowd:

"A hundred thousand people have come to the centre of Liverpool this afternoon. The authorities have allowed us to 'police' this hundred thousand ourselves. Why? Because they enjoy surrendering their power? Or because they're afraid of being trampled underfoot. There's a thin line between order and chaos. The police force of Liverpool may tread it this afternoon. A step wrong and the Mersey will rise a foot by nightfall, with largely innocent blood. We're gathered here today, peacefully, to demonstrate our determination to win this long and terrible battle against the employing classes and the state. What does that mean? Only this. All the transport workers of Liverpool are arm-in-arm against the enemy class.

We have sent a letter to the employers asking for an early settlement and a speedy return to work. If that brings no reply, if they ignore us, The Strike Committee advises a general strike.

In the face of the military and the police drafted into this city - and of the threat to bring gunboats into the Mersey - we can see nothing except a challenge. A challenge to every worker who values his job. A challenge to every claim each worker makes of his employer. A challenge to every right a worker should expect under common decency. Brothers, we rise to this challenge. And we meet it, head on."

There was a unanimous agreement to the strike even though most of the city was on strike anyway. Presumably this was to make it official.

Although everything so far was good natured, orderly, and peaceful the reasons for what happened next are hazy. Some reports state of a cart being overturned by the side entrance of St. George's Hall, or of Police attempting to remove some youths sitting on a window sill. Even then there is a different story of a man refusing to leave his vantage point of the window sill of the Station hotel in Lime Street as he watched the proceedings of the meeting. When the Police attempted to drag him down, the nearby crowd resented the show of force and fighting was meant to have ensued.

Even if that was the case it was no excuse to the actions of the Police who had gone against their agreement with Tom Mann by having one hundred soldiers from the Warwickshire regiment and numerous Police officers from Leeds and Birmingham.

Without warning the Police emerged from the hall and charged the crowd. The Police violently waved their batons and struck anybody who was in reach. It didn't matter whether it was men, women, or children they were viciously struck and knocked to the ground. Even then the blows were still struck even to those laying stricken like broken dolls on the floor.

An eyewitness described the scene 'as Policemen aiming cruel blows upon the heads of men, women, and children. Dozens lay bleeding and unconscious, citizens were to be seen lying helpless on the ground.'

In what seemed more of a battleground tactic the mounted horse Police were now ordered to charge and clear the steps and plateau of St. George's Hall. There were more screams of alarm as the full force of a cavalry horse charge hit the crowd and again struck anyone in the way. It took thirty minutes to clear the steps with the debris of broken glass, stones, bricks and people's belongings lost in the carnage being strewn across the plateau of St. George's Hall.

Some of the Police mainly from Birmingham were injured with one receiving a broken leg and another a head injury from being struck by an iron bar. This though paled into insignificance compared to the serious injuries of the public. Fred Bowers reports of how the aftermath represented a battlefield with the wounded lying in heaps. It was reported that one hundred and ninety-six were hospitalised and there were doubtless more who had severe injuries that were not reported. The Liverpool echo described it as 'a scene which reminded one of the turbulent times on Paris when the revolution was at its heights.'

By now the Liverpool stipendiary magistrate Stuart Deacon strolled out onto the steps of St. George's Hall and surrounded by troops read the Riot Act in order to clear the nearby streets of people otherwise the Police would do so.

Shock had turned to anger and now it was retaliation despite Tom Mann calling a halt to the proceedings. He was rightly fearful of what could happen next as he tried to get the crowd away, but this was in vain especially after the Police horses had led a cavalry charge.

Now fighting broke out across the city and it was in nearby Christian street that the brunt of the fighting took place. Rioters fought with police and troops with roof tiles being used as missiles to fight back against the authorities.

Deacon was again called to read the riot act as the police and troops tried to restore order. Although they had limited success with public houses being closed the fuse wire had been lit by the actions of the Police and troops as fighting continued to spread around the city.

Even now nobody knows who and why gave the orders for the baton and horse charge. There are many theories from incompetence, panic, or even more sinisterly whether it was deliberate to 'legitimately,' break down the strike and somehow restore order.

It was recorded that Pathé news had arranged to film Tom Mann's speech and had caught the Police charge on camera. The authorities fearful of the reaction that it would cause if it was shown quickly took the reels citing public safety. Even after the event the reels were not shown especially as awkward questions would be asked.

Trouble erupted during the night and the next couple of nights most notably around Great Homer street. It was a volatile time as there was fury that the authorities had appeared to provocatively use their superior force of Police and troops without any legitimate reason.

Most of the newspapers such as the Manchester Guardian condemned the 'merciless use of truncheons,' whilst the Times tried to pin the blame on the involvement of 'criminals and rioters,' plus sectarian conflicts.

Tensions were still high, and the stakes were to be raised much higher with the situation spiralling out of control for the authorities.

Undeterred by events the Liverpool strike committee as agreed, officially called a general strike from midnight on the 14th August 1911. On the following day the city was now at a standstill with the Liverpool Echo reporting 'that there was a quietness in the docks as workers heeded the call for strike action. The City Justices appealed for men to enrol as special constables and hundreds came forward to volunteer and were accepted.'

On the same day of the official strike, those that had been arrested during the previous days rioting were in a convoy of prisoners being escorted by thirty-two soldiers of the 18th Hussars on horseback, fully armed with live ammunition along with mounted Police. Due to the volatile nature of recent days it was deemed necessary and was justified in the sense that a crowd congregated to block the prison van. The intent was obvious as to why, when the crowd tried to break the prisoners out deeming that they had been unfairly arrested.

A magistrate who had been travelling with the five prison vans attempted to read out a copy of the riot act in order to dispel the crowd. The Liverpool Mercury reported that it took five attempts and 'that the troopers conscious of the importance of defending the prison vans had to defend their lives against the murderous onslaught being made on them from every side. At last the order to fire was given and five or six shots rang out in the air... But it was only a momentary halt to the proceedings. A man who been one of the foremost in the melee lunged forward towards one of the troopers; his arm was upraised and in his hand was a formidable iron bar. The trooper was not one of the men who had used his carbine but instantly realising that the moment was a deadly one for him, he quick as thought snatched his revolver from his holder and fired one shot just as arm wielding the fearsome weapon was falling upon him. It was a fatal aim the trooper had taken for his assailant fell mortally wounded.'

Two men John W. Sutcliffe and Michael Prendergast were killed. Four days later, on the 19th August two more civilians were shot by troops in Llanelli. This was the last occasion when British soldiers have killed civilians on the streets of mainland Britain.

Members of the strike committee distanced themselves from the disturbances stating that none of the men who had attacked the prison vans were strikers. Although both John Sutcliffe and Michael Prendergast did work on the docks. For the strike committee their focus was the dispute and putting pressure on the bosses to agree a deal.

With unrest still not easing up and the volatile mood that had engulfed the city it seemed that the authorities were getting more nervous and edgy. Reading the Liverpool Mercury report on the fatal killing during the crowds attempt to free the prisoners it sounded very much like a battle.

This seemed to be the view of the authorities who ordered anyone who belonged to the Liverpool Territorials to return the bolts of their rifles to the barracks which rendered the rifle useless. By doing this it eased the concern that if events escalated to a near meltdown then the weapons could not be used against the military or the Police.

Despite the show of force by the authorities it was still the Liverpool strike committee unofficially ran the city. It was starting to effect Britain's business due to the amount of trade that went in and out of Liverpool's sea ports.

With the strike committee only allowing essential items such as bread and milk to hospital out, with everything else at a standstill. Even the post that came in could not move without the committee's approval.

Panic and worry now beset the authorities who felt impotent at the current events. Anger was still on the street and there was a steely defiance from the strikers that they would not be broken. The authorities had lost control of the city and were increasingly alarmed that the disturbances on the street could lead to social revolution. The Lord Mayor of Liverpool expressed these fears to the Home Office 'declaring that a revolution was in progress, and that anarchy prevailed.'

It is why with three thousand and five hundred troops drafted in that the authorities were taking no chances. With events deteriorating every bit of force was viewed as being appropriate. Consequently, it must have been a shock for the inhabitants of Liverpool to slowly see two grey ships hovering in the distance. Eventually as they sailed closer to the docks, they were revealed to be two gunboats heading stealthily towards port.

These were not small gunboats with one of them HMS Antrim which weighed in at 11,020 tonnes and had the length of 473 feet and 6 inches. It could move at twenty-two knots (twenty-five miles per hour) and wasn't short of guns. Antrim had eighteen quick firing Hotchkiss guns, two submerged eighteen-inch torpedo tubes, and two, twelve pounder, eight cwt guns, which could also be dismantled and used ashore if needs be.

This was quite a surreal sight with the talk of what the gunboats were doing there and just as important whether the authorities were prepared to use them as the guns were pointed towards the city. Liverpool was in effect a city under siege as the authorities flexed their muscles like Goliath against David.

Officially no reason was given as to why two gunboats were sent up the Mersey on the 17th August 1911. It certainly may have been to show force and even wrest control of the docks if the situation deteriorated even more. As it was the two ships were there during the duration of the strike which caused a menacing shadow across the nearly completed Royal Liver building.

As Home Secretary Winston Churchill was held as responsible for sending the gunboats up the Mersey. Many at that time and certainly in parliament regarded him as an impulsive man prone to making rash decisions. Certainly, Churchill wanted to show the strikers that the authorities were prepared to use force as needs be and certainly had form as Home Secretary.

What is largely forgotten was that the actions of Churchill in Tonypandy, Liverpool, and other areas of the country that had industrial disputes disliked and distrusted Winston Churchill. Even after the second world war the mere mention of his name would be enough for someone to curse Churchill. A divisible man depending on which side of the fence you sat on and most certainly in that era.

M. Cole in 'growing up in the revolution,' gives a following account of the docks around that time of the strike. 'I remember the stench of the unscavenged streets – the corporation workers came out in sympathy- and of the truck loads vegetables rotting at Edge Hill station. I remember bits of broken bottle, relics of battles down by the docks, the rain patter of feet walking the pavements when the trams ceased to run and clank, the grey Antrim lying on guard in the Mersey, the soldiers marching through the streets, special editions of the evening editions of the evening papers coming out every half-hour, and American tourists decanted from the Baltic, sitting at the Pier Head on their Saratoga trunks with no porters to carry them away.'

Attempts were made to move essential freight and foodstuffs around the city in convoys guarded by special constables and troops. This though was only like applying a sticking plaster to a five-inch wound as the strike held firm.

With disturbances right across the country the ball was firmly in the strike committee's favour. The extra policing from areas such as Birmingham were recalled back home. However due to the railway strike they had to suffer the indignity of walking the forty miles to get the nearest train back to Birmingham. This again was another pressure point on the authorities as they were limited in being able to send Police and troops to trouble spots quickly and efficiently. Even then there were soldiers who were now deserting rather than face the prospect of having to fire on civilians.

If anything, the strike committee cranked it up another notch as Tom Mann announced a general strike of all transport workers. On the 17th August they were joined by tramway and corporation workers. In total there were now an estimated 66,000 on strike.

For the authorities they were now at breaking point. Resources were severely stretched due to other industrial disputes across the country and there was the fear that one of the major economic cities of the Empire was a powder keg away from erupting into a full revolt. This was fully emphasised with the infamous quote that Liverpool 'was the closest to revolution that they had seen.'

The only realistic option on the table for the authorities to stop the trouble and regain control of the city was that an agreement had to be reached. Maybe if Liverpool had not been such an influential city in terms of trade and supplying the rest of the country with food the authorities may just have tried to see if it could burn out. However, the strike committee were running the city and it was this that alarmed the authorities in case it did lead to an uprising and revolt, especially if there were any further deaths related to the dispute.

It was for this reason that Lloyd George persuaded the Prime Minister Asquith that an agreement had to be reached. An attempt had to be made to quell the unrest and especially Liverpool. So it was that the various bosses were told in no uncertain terms to bring an end to the strike.

This was not the news that they wanted to hear with the government having to quietly point out that policing and army resources were stretched. For Lloyd George the pragmatist it was the case of the bosses having to swallow a large and bitter slice of their pride to bring some order to the streets of Liverpool.

With a craw in the bosses throat the unions were asked to the table to sort out the grievances and more importantly end the dispute. The offer was immediately taken up by the trade unions who knew that they held a winning hand. It was essentially carte blanche for the strike committee and the trade union leaders. Nevertheless, it didn't stop fierce negotiations between the two parties when they met over the weekend of the 19th and 20th August at the Board of Trade in London.

As the strike that had brought Liverpool bosses to their knees was the railway strike, a deal was quickly agreed with the railwaymen going back to work on the 22nd August winning their concessions. To ensure more strength in the future, a new union was formed with the three unions being amalgamated and was called the National Union of railwaymen.

For the dockers they too had reached concessions, but the main prize was the agreement of the white book agreement. This set up a permanent joint committee to consider and agree proposed changes in working practices. To the employers they saw it as a way of heading off unofficial strikes whilst for some of the union officials it meant ensuring that there was discipline and control. Trade union recognition was another main agreement that had been a big bone of contention as the bosses had previously refused this demand.

Tom Mann expressed his views at the strikers victory declaring this statement to the press 'We are pleased indeed with the result. We have had a ten weeks fight and we have been through some very strenuous times. Allowing for the fact that we took on various sections of workers to help them ventilate their grievances and obtain redress and having fought for and won substantial improvements for the men who originally came out.'

For the bosses and the authorities there was a bitter taste in the mouth with some worried at the growing strength of the workers who were organising themselves into unions. The Times called the events in Liverpool as 'sinister and open to coercion and disorder.' It further went on to state that it was 'labour agitation gone mad... the situation appears to be rapidly and hopelessly from bad to worse. Anarchy reigns in the city.'

Despite Liverpool being brought to a standstill due to what was a general strike there was a threat to the agreement. Stupidly, the corporation had refused to reinstate the two hundred and fifty men who had been sacked when the tramway men went out. That refusal quickly crumbled when the strike committee stated that unless the men were reinstated then the strike would continue. Consequently, the corporation quickly capitulated and consented to the agreement of allowing the men to take back their jobs.

Once everything had been thrashed out and agreed the strike committee officially disbanded on the 24th August and with it the dispute which had lasted seventy-two days.

It still took a while for the city to get back to normality with sporadic attacks on conveys and trams. Plus, there were reports of witness intimidation for those who had been called to court as witnesses.

Due to the non-movement of perishable goods and rubbish that was left strewn across the street there was an epidemic of diarrhoea. The matter wasn't helped by the blockage of drains with a high rise of people passing away due to the poor sanitation.

Recognition of trade unionism was one of the main things to come from the dispute. Membership rose to a record high of fifty-one thousand in the NUDL. It also showed that workers were prepared to fight for better wages and conditions which would eventually lead to the rights now taken granted today. Social change was also another factor but that would take other events and further struggles for that to be realised.

Aftermath and legacy of the 1911 transport strike

Once the dust had started to settle down so too did the demands for a public enquiry. The coroner's inquest ruled that Michael Prendergast was shot by a member of the mob who had been seen firing rifles and exonerated the troop of Hussars. In the case of Sutcliffe, the jury gave a verdict of 'justifiable homicide,' citing that due to a dangerous riot all means necessary was required to restore order.

In terms of who and why the authorities gave the orders for the Police to charge a peaceful crowd at St. George's plateau this was never revealed. Leonard Dunning who had been the Chief Constable during the strike, retired not long after it had been resolved. The 1910-1911 report was delivered by his successor Francis Caldwell and the secrets stayed with Dunning even after his death.

Parliament did its best in closing the door on any awkward questions relating to the events in Liverpool and why two gunboats were sent up the Mersey. Rather than look to extend parliament they adjourned it on the 22nd August so no further questions could be raised whilst the events were still fresh in people's minds.

Even during the height of the crisis in Liverpool only two local MPs raised any questions relating to the strike. One was T.P. O'Connor the Nationalist for Liverpool Scotland road who questioned the Police brutality being enforced on the local population. Another was the Conservative MP Houston for West Toxteth who asked whether non-union members who wanted to work, could be moved around the city safely.

Winston Churchill himself ensured that there was a lack of publicity and brushed the events under the carpet. It was during this period that Churchill earned his infamous reputation amongst the working classes. Not just for sending gunboats up the Mersey, but troops firing on striking miners in Tonypandy and being used in Hull.

This period in history is scarcely covered with the 'Great Unrest,' seen as a mere blip. Roy Hattersley in his autobiography of David Lloyd George, titled the 'great outsider,' fully illustrates this view. Despite the justified grievances of the strikers in Wales and Liverpool, Hattersley states 'increases in the cost of living-which had combined with the militancy of the manual trade unions' leadership to precipitate the Tonypandy riots in 1910 -had continued into the following year.'

Hattersley continues to gloss over the events of Liverpool's transport strike with no mention of the gunboats being sent up the Mersey or 'bloody Sunday.' Again, there is the implication that the employer had reached an agreement and simply gives this about the events of August 1911 'Strikers rioted, troops were called in and, as was usual at the time, the government began to fear a red revolution.'

There seems to be a Downton Abbeyism of history of the benevolent Lord and rich employer doing the right thing for his workers who in turn were grateful and understood their station in life.

The reality is that people were becoming more politically aware and were quite prepared to be active if needs be. Tom Mann who helped lead the strike in Liverpool was a leading syndicalist but as Brian Towers in waterfront blues states 'the syndicalists were very pragmatic revolutionaries. As Taplin puts it the most that can be claimed is that workers adopted 'proto-syndicalist behaviour, that is forms of social action which lie between vague revolt and clear-cut revolutionary action.'

For the majority of strikers' they were not 'raving revolutionaries' intent on bringing down the state. Simply put they just wanted to be paid and treated fairly. Even the Liverpool Daily Post had this to say once the strike had ended 'if the ship owners had been more sympathetic in dealings with the workforce the problem could have been resolved.'

In terms of modern and social history the events of 1911 deserve to be heard. Although the primary aim was to obtain better wages, conditions, and trade union recognition it was the first steps to introducing better working rights, social conditions, housing, and the emergence of the NHS.

None of the above was given easily and every inch had to be fought. The strikers in the 1911 transport strike had to endure the violence of the Police and troops as seen in the baton charge at St. George's Hall plateau. Added to which the authorities flexed their muscles further by sending two gunboats up the Mersey in what could only be seen as to intimidate the city occupants.

Nevertheless, and despite the hardships the strikers remained firm and well organised. It was why the strike was a success and the altruistic motives alarmed the authorities and even some elements within their own trade union leadership.

At the height of the dispute it was the strike committee that ran the city. For anything to move in or out of the docks they had to have an approved pass from the said committee. It was for this reason that the authorities feared that this could be the start of a social revolution if it continued. This was why the government of Asquith put pressure on the employers to make a deal and to do it as quickly as possible.

Whether it could have led to a revolution if the strike had gone on any longer is debatable. It could quite easily have become more bloodied with fighting in the streets but what must be remembered if the authorities had not attacked the crowd without any provocation then the trouble afterwards may not have happened. However, the authorities still had the troops on their side and the priority of the strike committee was not revolution but better pay and rights.

After the strike had concluded the trust between the authorities, police and the local populace was low. It wasn't helped that the Liverpool city council agreeing to give £2000 to Police Officers who had been injured during the dispute.

Of course, the authorities and the bosses regained control after the dispute, but it was still a significant event in the labour movement. After all it is better to take one slice of cake and come back for another piece rather than trying to take the lot and ending up with nothing.

Trade Union membership rose to record levels with the NUDL seeing a fifty-one thousand members at its peak. Naturally this was due to the success of the strike but awareness that a strong union meant they had more strength in terms of future disputes and negotiations.

In terms of historical importance, it is highly significant. Economically, Liverpool was just as important as London was in terms of trade. The strike was an important event but equally for more rights and social improvement. It may not have come straight away but this was fight that would continue in the years to come.

Harry Leslie Smith the activist and author of numerous books such as 'Harry's last stand,' who sadly passed away in 2018, was more than aware of the hard battle it took to provide a better life of working rights, the creation of the welfare state and the health service. That's why it is important to remember and learn from social events such as the 1911 transport strike lest in the words of Harry Leslie Smith who said 'do not let my past, become your future.'

Crowds congregate in support of the transport strike, St. George's Plateau, 13th August 1911.' It later became known as 'Bloody Sunday,' when for reasons unknown, the Police charged the crowd.

The crowd jostling for position to listen to Tom Mann and show support for the strike.'

'Strikers, leading the fightback.' At one point the strike committee ran
Liverpool in the summer of 1911.

'SEND THE GUNBOATS UP THE MERSEY,' AFTER RIOTS BREAK OUT
AFTER BLOODY SUNDAY, THE AUTHORITIES TRY TO RESTORE
CONTROL BY SENDING HMS ANTRIM AND ANOTHER GUNBOAT UP
THE MERSEY.'

1919 THE YEAR OF NEAR REVOLUTION

Eight years after the 1911 transport strike, Britain was still reeling from the aftershock of the First World War. Back in August 1914 there was a patriotic fever of men joining the army to do their bit for 'King and country.' Alfred Leete's, Lord Kitchener poster of his finger pointing with it declaring 'Your country needs you,' was one of the best marketing posters as thousands signed up in their droves. Many believed that the war would be over by Christmas and wanted their chance to be a hero. Even being underage didn't deter some with the recruiting sergeant turning a blind eye.

The Great war as it was called, quickly turned into a nightmare of mud, rats, and slaughter of thousands. A stalemate ensued of trench warfare which seemed to grind on for eternity. War was the dark shadow that was cast over everybody. Nobody was immune from its bony fingers. From losing family, friends, being wounded, and living with the continual noise of guns and the constant fear of death.

When the armistice was declared at the eleventh hour on the eleventh day of November 1918 there was relief that the fighting was now at an end. Much had changed within those four years. Russia had overthrown Tsar Nicholas II with Germany's Kaiser Wilhelm II abdicating on the 9th November 1918. The Austro-Hungary Empire had collapsed with the map distinctly looking different as new countries emerged from the shattered remains.

Nothing was the same in Britain as the Empire was entering its death throes as its influence waned in the world. There was already open rebellion in Ireland and rumblings of discontent in India. Added to which there were the oilfields of Mosul, (modern day Iraq) which needed troops to keep control.

For the people back home, it was a case of trying to find work and to get back to normality as soon as possible. It could also be said there was a feeling of political awareness with the Government very much fearful of a Bolshevik uprising happening in Britain. Consequently, it was also a period of tension, fear, nervousness and anger that after fighting for their country they were struggling to meet ends meet.

The Liberals had won a landslide as their leader David Lloyd George had promised a 'land fit for heroes,' and for demobilisation to happen as quickly as possible.

Some such as Field Marshall Henry Wilson damned Lloyd George for 'vote catching,' which had helped win the election for the Liberals. Troops were still needed not just while the peace treaty was still to be ratified but to keep the British colonies secure.

There were also those in the establishment that were fearful of mass demobilisation at once. With the tremors of the Russian revolution and the upheaval in Europe still being felt, some felt that it could be a recipe for disaster.

For those looking at the bigger picture they realised that there would be masses of men searching for work all at once with the chance that unemployment could rise. Dissatisfaction could lead to violence and if harnessed could possess a real danger of overthrowing the elite. These were men who were not only trained to fight but had lived each day in the mud and trenches knowing that they might be killed at any minute.

Furthermore, they were battle hardened and after being subject to the harshest discipline where falling asleep on guard duty could result in the death penalty, they might feel that they had nothing to lose. Lloyd George had declared 'a land fit for heroes,' and a return to bleak poverty might see some decide that it was time for change.

To complicate matters even further, Winston Churchill had become obsessed with the Bolshevik threat in the sense that the events of Russia could influence a domino effect in Britain. With the fledgling government led by Lenin, Churchill thought this was the right opportunity to strike and break up the threat of Bolshevism. However, there was a bit of a flaw in that thought, namely the conscripts, troops, and civilians who did not want to suffer any more killing and war. For the soldiers they didn't want to spend another minute longer than necessary in their uniform. Consequently, they were not too happy at the prospect of fighting in another land that they had no business to be in.

With the war over, 1919 was a year of uncertainty and what the future might bring. These feeling spilt onto the streets with people fed up of unemployment, poor conditions, and in some respects made them politically aware. Add to the fact that there was the paranoia of a red revolution engulfing the government it wasn't surprising that any dispute or trouble was heavy handed.

This was the year of Glasgow and 'red Clyde,' as people came out to support more employment, race riots, a national Police strike that saw riots breaking out and another gunboat sent up the Mersey. Troops were sent out on the street and there was fear that the army could not be controlled as mutinies broke out amongst the ranks.

Red flags flew proudly and put the wind up the Government which incidentally became the symbol of red Clyde. For the authorities, revolution was only a riot or gunfire away from an open revolt. After all the world had been turned upside down and although Germany had surrendered, it didn't mean that the masses might turn on them like they did in Russia.

The first problems occurred in the army which had been simmering especially after the promise of demobilisation. As we shall see the government's handling of the events was poor and jittery as they either didn't react to events or simply came in heavy handed as we see below.

Disgruntlement and mutinies in the army

Fresh after the armistice in November 1918 the first post-war mutiny was at a camp in Shoreham. The trigger had been the mistreatment of a soldier which had led to a mass walk out of seven thousand troops who marched to Brighton town hall.

Their demands were immediate demobilisation and after refusing to return to their posts after a General was sent from London an agreement was made that one thousand troops could be immediately be demobilised with more to follow over the coming year.

It could be argued that this was the first mistake from the authorities to cave in so easily. Once word spread of what at happened at Shoreham it could encourage soldiers that disobedience was the way to get demobilised quicker.

There was also disgruntlement as the authorities gave no real thought to what the mood of the men was. For example, the army decreed that those to be in 'pivotal jobs,' were to be demobilised first. As these would be the men who were the last to be called up it seemed to be last in, first out. This of course led to anger for those who had served longer.

As 1918 entered the end of the year, resentment was simmering after troops who had been in active service in France were granted leave for Christmas. The consensus was that they would be demobilised once they arrived back in Britain in time for the holidays. Rather than being sent back to civvy street they received orders that once their leave was over that they had to return to Folkstone and be sent back to France.

The mood was already sour as they arrived in Folkstone at the prospect of taking a boat to France rather than being demobbed. No information had been given either as to when they could expect to be released from the army. Added to which nothing had been done to resolve the complaints of poor food and excessive officer privileges.

More anger broke out when rumours started to circulate that some of the men would be sent to fight in Russia to fight in the words of Winston Churchill 'the baboonery of Bolshevism.'

For many the last thing they wanted to be involved in was another bloody conflict that had seen so many killed. Putting their lives on the line yet again in a foreign land was not something that they wanted to do. Especially as they had no quarrel with the Russian people.

It was this that led to two thousand troops taking over the port declaring that no military vessels would be allowed to set sail. The Daily Herald had this to say about the events. 'On their own signal-three taps of a drum- two thousand men, unarmed and in perfect order demonstrated the fact that they were fed up – absolutely fed up. Their plan of action had been agreed upon the night before: no military boat should be allowed to leave Folkestone for France that day or any day until they were guaranteed their freedom.'

Pickets were set up and as more soldiers came into Folkestone, they were invited to join the strike. Many did and by Saturday the 4th January, ten thousand soldiers without any officers in charge, ran the quayside. Orders now came from the committees that had been set up. It was outright mutiny with only Canadians and Australian soldiers allowed to sail if they wanted to. Not surprisingly not many did.

One officer tried to interfere and quash the mutiny but received some rough house treatment for his troubles. So much so that he pleaded 'I am a relative of Douglas Haig.' That though didn't cut much ice with the mutineers who sent him away packing.

In the meantime, alarm bells were ringing within the Government who could see their authority evaporating in front of them. Over ten thousand troops marched through the town with the townspeople showing their support as they came out to applaud them. According to the Herald they had arranged a mass meeting at mid-day and formed a soldiers' union.

With the soldiers taking control and becoming well organised, the government had although alarmed knew that they had to tread carefully, lest one wrong move saw the same outcome in Germany or Russia.

An attempt had been made to put down the mutiny down with the Fusiliers being sent in carrying bayonets and ball cartridges. One rifle made to go up, but a picket seized it with the Fusiliers stepping back.

It was an awkward situation for the authorities who couldn't be seen to give in so readily to the mutinies but by keeping dissenting soldiers together who were also armed they could see that it had the potential to escalate into violence and revolution.

The job of trying to resolve the mutiny was given to General Sir William Robertson who was the Commander in Chief of the Home forces. His modus operandi was to resolve the matter as quickly and discreetly as possible. After discussions with the picket leaders he promised no reprisals and an extension of leave. With regards to the demobilising of troops this was accelerated to ensure most of the troops who went out on strike were discharged from the army.

If the authorities hoped that the mutinies would burn out it continued to burn as fierce as a strong wind accelerates a grass fire. Dover saw another mutiny erupt with men from the army service corps marching straight down to Downing street on the 6th January after they were told that they would be the last to be demobilised. Four days it was agreed that most of the soldiers who had protested were discharged from the army.

For the Government it was turning into a nightmare in the sense on whether they could now trust the army. As seen in 1911, soldiers had been used to quash discontent and industrial disputes. If there were more industrial disputes like the Liverpool transport strike or further mutinies turned violent, then who could they rely on to break them down? It didn't help that the Police's loyalty was also being questioned after going on strike in 1918 and quickly winning their demands.

For some it seemed that Bolshevism was now on their doorsteps and just needed a spark to set it off in motion like it did in Russia. Europe was still unsettled which caused the establishment to be even more jittery that it could spread to British shores. News had arrived of more political disturbances in

Berlin as members of the Spartacist movement declared the creation of the German Soviet republic. As it was the army which is always key in such matters were loyal to the newly formed republic. The revolt was ruthlessly put down. It showed the British Government how vital it was that they retained the loyalty of the army.

The first attempt at trying to curb the mutinies came when over five thousand soldiers in the port of Southampton went on strike with committees set up. Again, the issue was of demobilisation as the troops thought they would be discharged rather than being sent to France with no indication of when they would be demobbed. They also had the support of the local people who knew precisely what the soldiers were going through. After all everybody had a loved one or a family member who they wanted to see back home from the army. For them the war was over, and they had done their bit. Now was the time for the soldiers to return home permanently and try to re-build their lives.

General Sir William Robertson who had negotiated a peaceful resolution in Folkstone sent General Hugh Trenchard to deal with the matter in any way fit. He was very much a man who felt that no compromise should be met therefore was viewed as the ideal person to lay a mark across the sand.

Trenchard was the man that had been put in charge of the Royal flying corps during the war and was also the founder of the Royal Air Force. His actions though showed what he thought of the ordinary soldiers and the working population. To him there was a hierarchy which should be obeyed unquestionably.

After arriving at the camp, Trenchard had a meeting with the commander of the camp were the troops were mutinying. Trenchard was not impressed with what he had to say and how the commander had handled the mutiny. As far as he was concerned the man was weak and inept. All it needed was an authoritative figure like himself to put this nonsense to bed.

Trenchard though was to be sorely mistaken and severely underestimated the anger of the men. After being driven down to docks with his aide-de-camp Maurice Baring he demanded to speak and address the thousands of soldiers within the docks.

The gate was about as far as Trenchard got as he was jeered and cat-called as he tried to gain access. Despite the taunts and heckles Trenchard still believed that his seniority would carry some clout as he attempted to order the men back and to put an end to this 'bolshy nonsense.'

Even when Trenchard was still being loudly shouted down and jostled he still didn't take the hint that his words meant nothing, so the men took matters into their own hands. Annoyed at the arrogance and pig headedness of the man they grabbed hold of Trenchard and roughly ejected him out of the docks 'telling him to stay out,' and to only come back when he was prepared to listen to the men's grievances.

Once Trenchard was back to his own base he was furious at the treatment that was meted out to him. He later complained that the men were not prepared to listen to him and was shocked at being roughly manhandled. Consequently, with Trenchard's pride taking a bruising he was prepared to ignore the higher echelons of Southern England by seeking military assistance. The General Officer of the Southern Command instructed Trenchard to 'not open fire under circumstances,' but was coldly ignored by Trenchard. Instead he replied that he was not seeking anyone's permission for what he was about to do, especially as Trenchard was a higher rank.

For Trenchard knew that the men at the docks were not armed and was quite happy to initiate a bloodbath to restore order to reassert the authority that he had been commanded to do. As far as Trenchard was concerned he had given the men the chance to end the mutiny and had not taken the opportunity to do so.

After commandeering two hundred and fifty soldiers who Trenchard felt were trustworthy he returned to the camp and ordered his troops to cock their weapons and to fire on his word of command. For the mutineers present they were not in the slightest doubt that Trenchard would open fire. This was a not bluff especially as they were unarmed

Once more Trenchard attempted to address the crowd to restore order and after a sergeant shouted an obscenity he was quickly grabbed by the military police. The majority of men now crumbled with only one hundred left who had barricaded themselves in. Trenchard ended it by ordering his troops to smash the windows and to turn the water hoses to be turned on them.

With the mutiny now ended, Trenchard identified who he felt were the ringleaders and were taken away to be charged. Churchill warmly congratulated Trenchard on his 'masterly handling of the Southampton riots.'

This though wasn't the end of protests within the army. Indeed, the Government was highly anxious on the units on whom they could trust. With industrial unrest on the horizon they wanted to know who they could rely on to restore public order if it came down it. If the units that were sent down refused or even joined the strikers or protestors, then it could lead to the collapse of the establishment.

Every unit was to report weekly on the mood of their men. Some of the questions asked the following:

Will troops in various areas respond to orders for assistance to preserve the public peace?

Will they assist in strike breaking?

Will they parade for draft to overseas, especially to Russia?

There were also questions about political activism such as Trade Unionism or the formation of soldiers' councils.

It showed the concerns that the government had over retaining the loyalty of their soldiers. With worries of industrial unrest and the fear of Bolshevism, the last thing that they wanted was unrest within the army. As seen in history the success of any revolution relied on the army supporting the revolt. With mutinies breaking out it was uncertain times indeed.

With the mutiny in Southampton being put to bed it must not have helped the Government's jitters when another high-profile mutiny took place at the port of Calais. In some respects, it was a lot more serious due to the Calais troops having access to weapons.

Again, it was the issue of demobilisation, the poor conditions, and the over use of privileges of the Officers. News was received that the men from the Royal Ordnance and the Army Service Corps were refusing to operate the ports. Not only that but they had joined forces with French workers to bring the railways and shipping to a halt. With front line troop units refusing orders this was another difficult moment for the Government.

The spark of the mutiny was the arrest of Private John Pantling of the Royal army corps who was accused by the authorities of delivering a 'seditious speech,' to an assembly of soldiers. It was in reaction to the poor conditions and as had been the case the senior officers were ordered to take a firm line against any dissident behaviour.

It was a move that enraged Pantling's fellow soldiers who felt that he had only been airing the truth about their grievances. Furthermore, they viewed it as their commanding officers not even attempting to listen to them.

So it was that on pay night the men at Val de Lievre decided to make a jail break and release John Pantling. To restore authority, the officers attempted to re-arrest Pantling and brought in more military Police. That though failed badly as it only infuriated the men further that the Commanding Officer had to relent and agree to meet the men.

Not wanting to stand still the soldiers organised the camps into soldiers' councils called the Calais soldiers and sailors association. It was a decision well made by the mutineers as the Officers attempted to end the mutiny by re-arresting Pantling. Whatever the reasons why they decided to take this course action is unclear especially as it was the equivalent of throwing petrol on a fire and not expecting it to blow up higher flames.

Considering that the Russian and German armies had set up similar army councils that led to the fall of the monarchy in both countries it was a fool hardy scheme to re-arrest Pantling and antagonise the men further.

On cue the soldiers' councils called a strike and not a single man turned up when reveille was called in the morning with sentries now replaced by pickets. The authorities had now lost control of the camps in Calais as other soldiers came out in solidarity. Nothing could go in or out without the soldiers say so.

The councils had now taken the name of the 'Calais soldiers and sailors association,' with other camps quickly adopting the title. With the French troops also supporting the strikers it was very much clear as to who was now in charge.

Pantling was now released but it was too little and too late as matters had gone too far with the demands of immediate demobilisation being called for.

This of course was not good for the authorities. Although the war had ended it was only an armistice and lest talks broke down then troops would be needed to be mobilised for war. Not only that but with industrial unrest back home and the Russian revolution still fresh in the minds there was a panic of how this could spread back to Britain and start an uprising there. It was not for nothing that the Calais mutiny was referred to as the 'Calais Soviet.'

It was vital therefore that the Calais mutiny was swiftly put down and to make an example of the men that were involved. That was the orders that the Commander in Chief of the British Forces in France, Field Marshall Douglas Haig gave to General Sir Julian Byng. The mutiny was to be put down by any means necessary.

It didn't start well for Byng whose arrival was delayed due to French railway workers going out in support of the soldiers' strike. To add salt into the wounds Byng's car was immediately commandeered by the mutineers when he did arrive ahead of his own units.

When Byng's troops did eventually arrive, he had them set up strategic points with guns set up around the camp, ready to open fire if required. Tensions were quite high within the higher echelons as to whether this could blow up into a full revolt.

There are two different versions of how the Calais mutiny was resolved. Simon Webb in his book '1919 Britain's year of revolution,' states that due to the overwhelming show of force the mutineers surrendered. Four were arrested as ringleaders with Byng wanting them shot for mutiny only for Winston Churchill to overrule the decision with the four men given long prison terms.' There was a fear that executing the mutineers would just rekindle the dispute and turn more violent. Churchill wanted it to put to bed with no further chances of repercussions.

Whereas 'Mutinies,' by Dave Lamb and the Libcom website state that in the words of one of the mutineers Byng's troops were 'bits of boys who were sent out just as the war ended.' They too didn't really want to be there with some even joining the mutineers. This was certainly true as there are accounts of some of Byng's men feeling they had more in common with the strikers

In the meantime, it was agreed that Pantling would be court-martialled whilst the mutineers were in control and his acquittal would be binding. By doing this, the mutineers knew that once the strike was over there was no chance of the verdict being quashed. They were quite wise to do so as the authorities reluctantly agreed seeing that they didn't hold the cards.

Following a conference with Byng and other senior officers, major concessions were agreed with better quality and quantity of food being increased. Added to which, promises were made that officers would not be allowed to sell their rations to the locals which had infuriated the men.

For Lamb the Calais mutiny came to a close after a surprise vote by the council ruled in favour of calling an end to the dispute.

Webb was correct that there were repercussions for the ring leaders and that Churchill had overruled the original verdict of execution. Certainly, it was difficult for Byng to regain control not just due to the delay but the quality of soldiers. Most were young conscripts who didn't really want to be there.

Added to which the mutineers had total control of Calais with its strike committees.

The truth no doubt is probably somewhere in the middle of both versions. Certainly, Byng had the strategic position and enough troops to open fire on the mutineers. However as the men had won in terms of concessions and the release of Pantling, what more could be possibly gained especially as there was the threat of bloodshed?

In regards as to what happened to Pantling this is not mentioned by Lamb or Libcom. According to the website a century of stories and 'the unknown army,' states that after suffering six days in leg chains in a cold prison, Malcolm Pantling died of influenza two weeks after being released. Four days short of this thirty third birthday.

By now matters were worsening for Lloyd George's Government as a strike in Clyde was feared to be the start of a Bolshevik uprising. Hence the nickname that it was to become known as the 'red Clyde,' dispute when a red flag was raised.

As there was anxiety and uneasiness over whether they could fully trust their own soldiers the authorities made enquiries as to whether there were any regiments that they could fully trust. The response was that they could rely on the Guards (Coldstream, Welsh, Irish, Scots, and Grenadier guards). They were advised by the army top brass that they would obey orders without question and could be trusted not to fraternise with the strikers. Ironically the first event that they were summoned to break was a soldiers' strike that was taking place in London.

The mood was already black when the troops had been told to report at London to be ready to be dispatched to France. It also didn't help that there were rumours that some of them would be sent to fight in Russia. Despite this being the basis of some of the mutinies the authorities certainly didn't seem to learn from them. Again the majority of the men were annoyed that they would not be demobbed any time soon.

As ordered the soldiers arrived at Victoria station in London, ready to be deployed on the next trains which would take them to the nearest ports to set sail for France.

Considering that the senior officers must have had an inkling about the bad feeling amongst the men, it was rather foolish to tell the troops that they had to sort out their own accommodation and food when no trains were available for that day. Fed up and annoyed that they were not even being provided for, they took umbrage with their officers and let them know in no uncertain terms that they were not happy at the lack of support and assistance.

With tempers escalating like the tremors of a volcano getting ready to erupt the senior officer wired through for the Scots Guards to put any potential revolts to bed. Due to the seriousness of the situation the Scots Guards arrived quickly who surrounded and disarmed the men before marching them to Wellington barracks to be arrested.

This though was not the end of matter as another group who had witnessed the scenes at Victoria station had promptly formed into marching order and made their way towards parliament. Fed up that there was no sign that they were being demobbed, the conditions, and now the fiasco of the men having to fend for themselves due to the lack of transport they were going to vent their anger personally to the Government.

More alarmingly it wasn't just a handful of soldiers but over a thousand men. It was more than enough to worry the Government that this might break out into a full revolt, especially as they were fully armed and furious at how they were being treated.

Glancing through the window Churchill must have thought this was the start of an uprising when he saw the soldiers with their rifles at the slope. Worried about the consequences that the man responsible for the army was seen he quickly backed away from the window. He later declared in his memoirs that during that turbulent day that 'I remained in my room, a prey to anxiety.'

It was at this point that Churchill rang Major General Sir Geoffrey Feilding wanting to know which units were available to deal with the mutiny. He replied that there was a reserve battalion of Grenadier Guards and two troops of Household cavalry at his disposable. Pausing, with the tightness in his chest, Churchill asked if it came down to the crunch would these troops obey orders. Feilding replied that he had no question about their loyalty.

By now the troops had moved on to Horse Guard Parade where the crowd got agitated and angry as a civil servant attempted to address the crowd. They wanted someone higher up the chain who could make guarantees not just pass their concerns on.

The Grenadier guards now moved into position as they strategically placed machine guns to let the striking soldiers know that they were surrounded. It was then that orders were given for the Household cavalry to move forward from one direction as more guards with bayonets drawn moved forward slowly ready to attack their fellow soldiers if ordered.

Since the striking troops were also armed the tension could have been cut by a knife. All it needed was someone firing a rifle and it could quite easily have turned into a bloodbath as the Grenadier guards had the troops surrounded in a pincer movement.

With the guards slowly approaching the troops with orders to surrender, the troops saw that they were surrounded with no place to move, surrendered and allowed themselves to be arrested. It was only by the skin of their teeth that the authorities had managed to avert a bloodbath.

The authorities certainly didn't want it to linger or allow resentment to build up. Consequently, the incidents were brushed under the carpet with no court martial for the troops involved. After all the authorities did not want a martyr for the troops to rally to. Instead the striking troops that were involved were quickly dispatched to France as originally planned.

Not that this was the end of the tetchiness within the Government who were twitchy at any possible militancy. After all, even the soldiers who had been demobbed had seen action and some of those were regarded as revolutionary, with some at the forefront of political protests. Basil Thomson, who was Director of Intelligence in 1919, spoke of his anxiety of former and current soldiers who had whole heartedly accepted the Soviet idea. Most notably the 'sailors, soldiers, and airmen, union.'

Tension was high especially due to the industrial and general unrest of that year and after. If the Government could not rely on their last resort of the army to nip any disturbances in the bud, then any protests could be the flame hissing along the gunpowder trail and see the establishment fall.

Consequently, the plans to invade Russia was quietly removed from the table not just for the logistics but that their own troops wanted no more blood and just wanted to be demobbed. Winston Churchill's influence was pulled after a speech by Lloyd George relating to no plans involving Russia. It was a move that had taken Churchill by surprise but Lloyd George like many others thought Churchill was turning into a liability and even a threat to Lloyd George's job.

These were turbulent times for Lloyd George and his government with more protests and strikes continuing within that year.

Red Clyde

If there was one event in 1919 that probably shook the Government and make them wonder if a revolution was imminent then it was the events that took place in Glasgow. The images of strikers defiantly marching with red flags on poles being hoisted high must have seen a few pale faces in authority. Certainly, it only convinced the Government that this was the start of a Bolshevik uprising that troops and tanks were sent onto to the street.

What caused the dispute was more to do with an altruistic attitude to spread employment by reducing the working week from fifty-four hours to a forty-hour week. By doing this it meant that the work could easily be shared around. It was a move that the STUC, Glasgow Trades and Labour Council as well as other trade unions who also endorsed this view.

Despite Lloyd George's claim of a 'land fit for heroes,' poverty was high and finding work was high. It was hardly surprising that after surviving the bloodied mud of the trenches that resulted in over sixteen million deaths that there was anger at how they were casually discarded.

The proposal of reducing   working hours fell on deaf ears from the employer so the only way to move forward was a proposal for a forty-hour strike which was called for on the 27th January 1919. Support for this was unanimous with the Glasgow Herald stating that there was over forty thousand people on strike.

Like the mutinies that occurred and the previous disputes in 1911 it was the fact that it was ran and organised by the workers. The very fact that they were willing to share the work, with some prepared to take a cut in wages to ensure employment for everyone was a move that puzzled and upset the establishment. For them it stank of the bogeyman that was Bolshevism.

As far as they were concerned it was very much a hierarchal structure from the Monarchy at the top to the workers at the bottom. Even then there was still a structure whether it was a manager or foreman. Everybody had their place and to go against it went against what they believed was a civilised society.

When there was disputes it was done with Trade Union officials so when the workers organised themselves, ignored their own trade unions and presented their demands to the employers as a united body.

It was this more than anything that frightened the establishment especially as this had erupted in another industrial dispute in Belfast. For Lloyd George and his government this was not for the workers to worry about employment but for Westminster to be concerned and attempt to resolve.

An altruistic view by the strikers was totally alien and many high up in Government believed it to be a Bolshevist plot ready to overthrow the Government. Russia was still fresh in the minds and Germany had their own uprising with the Kaiser abdicating plus a failed Bolshevist revolt. Strong action it was felt was needed to put this uprising down.

Glasgow had recently witnessed some marches with one occasion seeing some 10,000 people marching from St Andrews Halls to the City chambers. Most frighteningly, for those who feared a Bolshevik revolt, there were some protestors proudly waving red flags. By Friday the 31st January over 60,000 were on strike.

It was a mood that was summed by Mr Cameron of the Discharged Soldiers Federation who had addressed the marchers at the city chambers by declaring 'they had fought for their country and now wanted to own it.' For some this was a chance to make real changes and let the authorities know what their views were.

With emotions running high it saw the local newspapers summing up the fear of the establishment as the Glasgow Herald referred to the strikers and their techniques as 'the methods of terrorism.' The Scotsman's headline was 'Terrorism on the Clyde.' The Times had some sympathy for the workers but believed that they had been misled by 'a gang of revolutionaries,' who were exploiting them.

To them these were the three firebrands in question Manny Shinwell, Davie Kirkwood, and Neil Maclean. These were the men according to the Times 'who have challenged the Government.'

To try and resolve the situation the committee of strikers asked Glasgow's Lord Provost to intervene on their behalf with the Government. James Stewart said that he would investigate it and for the committee to come back on Friday 31st January.

Notices had been put up requesting strikers to be there with the Strike Bulletin declaring for all strikers to be at St. George's Square at 12.30pm 'Be in time and be there.'

The square was full of strikers and protestors. Estimates of the crowd varied from sixty thousand to one hundred thousand. A defiant mood crackled amongst the crowd as men shimmied up lamps with some unfurling red flags to raise the stakes even higher.

Winston Churchill was already preparing himself for trouble by talking about 'going gently at first we should get the support of the nation, and then the troops could be used effectively,' whilst declaring that some of the leaders should be seized.

At the same war cabinet meeting the Secretary of State for Scotland decried that this was a 'Bolshevist rising,' and needed to be smashed.

In order to alleviate the concerns, the Deputy Chief of the Imperial General Staff advised that six tanks and a hundred motor lorries with drivers were heading up north that night by rail. All of which would be used if called upon.

A discussion was also made about whether the strike leaders should be arrested and prosecuted but decided against it for the time being. The only reason for that was they did not want to inflame the situation and hereby make the strikers feel that they were being oppressed by arresting their leaders.

Tension was certainly deep within the Government who could see parallels with Russia. It was a serious situation that needed to be handled carefully. They had already contended with mutinies and other industrial disputes which were still simmering despite being resolved. Nervously, they must have wondered whether this was the powder keg ready to go off. Could they handle a potential revolt if it did kick off it or would it spread further south? Also, could the army be trusted?

For the strikers this was not foremost in their minds as a striker Harry McShane said later 'We didn't regard the Forty Hours Strike as a revolution. We saw it more as the beginning of things to come.'

There are some instances where the lessons of the past are not learnt. After Peterloo and more recently the 1911 Transport strike in Liverpool, the Police decided to make a baton charge on civilians waiting on George Street.

As agreed, Neil Maclean, Shinwell, Davie Kirkwood and Harry Chambers went to meet the Lord Provost to see what the Government had offered. To show their support a crowd of thousands congregated outside ready to hear what the outcome of the meeting.

No warning was given when the Police made a full-scale baton charge as they violently hit anyone in their range indiscriminately. Nobody really knows who gave the order or the reasons why but as the Glasgow Herald stated 'men, women, and children were felled in the melee that followed.'

By now panic ensued as people tried to flee the attack of the Police. There was screams of men, women, and children as bodies fell either by being hit or being swallowed up by the crowd. As some fell back there was quickly anger and outrage as members of the crowd sought to protect themselves and others by fighting back. Missiles of bottles and stones were launched with some obtained by a truck stuck in North Frederick street.

With trouble breaking out the Sheriff who was called Mackenzie attempted to read the riot act to disperse the crowd, but had it ripped out of his hand by a striker. According to the records, Mackenzie still finished it by memory, but it was immaterial as scarcely anybody listened to him.

There was also another dispute over the involvement of Davie Kirkwood who was accused of agitating and encouraging the crowd to be more violent. A Police Officer at the trial of the Strike leaders which took place at the High Court Edinburgh, declared that Kirkwood had shouted 'never mind their batons, get into them,' as he urged the crowd to get stuck into the Police.

This contrasted with the Town Clerk who told the court that he was doing his best to calm the crowd down and had actually said 'this is not the opportune time for us; our time will come.'

What wasn't in doubt according to many eyewitnesses was that as Davie Kirkwood rushed out of the chambers to see what the commotion was, ended up being knocked unconscious by a Police baton. To back up this evidence a nearby photographer had taken a vote of Kirkwood laying stricken on the floor. Willie Gallagher and Shinwell were also arrested with Kirkwood for inciting trouble.

By now though the fighting had spread right throughout the centre of Glasgow. One Sergeant described how he and an inspector were pinned against the wall as they were pelted with stones. Another Constable had described the scenes being worse than when he had served in the war in France.

Up by Cathedral street it appeared that the Police had lost control as they tried to flee the crowd. Whipped up into a frenzy they even pulled escaping Policemen from the wall where one witness said that they had taken one hell of a hiding.

Tension was rising like a high-stake poker game as the authorities debated what to do next. It seemed that the Police had lost control and were fearful that a revolt had broken out as red flags were raised high. The Daily Record reported that some of the crowd were singing the 'red flag,' song with some fearful that Glasgow was to suffer the same fate as Russia did in 1917.

It was why they decided that the army ought to be called in to help quash the spark of revolt lest it spiralled out of control. Consequently, the authorities decided that troops had to be sent in to assist the Police if needs be.

Nevertheless, there was still a touch of caution as to which soldiers should be used. Therefore, it was deemed too risky to use the Scottish troops in Maryhill barracks in case they refused to hurt their own and decide that they had more in common with the protestors and join them in the revolt.

To ensure that this didn't happen troops from outside of Scotland were used to quell the dispute, whilst the local soldiers were confined to barracks. Harry McShane spoke that the men were aggressive as he tried to explain the situation to marching troops. 'They were quite prepared to use their weapons,' McShane recalled. 'I'll always remember one of them pointing to his rifle and saying this is better than bottles.'

In a show of strength and attempt to subdue the protestors, tanks were now sent onto the streets of Glasgow. For the casual observer looking at the pictures one would think that a full-scale war had broken out as troops and tanks patrolled the streets.

Machine guns were even positioned across parts of the city on top of buildings such as in George Square. Even the city chambers had a howitzer placed there.

The language of the local media sounded more like a war or that revolution had broken out. One paper called 'the bulletin,' showed two soldiers in tin hats with fixed bayonets and described them as 'this formidable guard-equal in strength to the guard at the bridge-end of the Rhine.'

Harry McShane dismissed any potential threat by stating that 'there was no open threat and we learned to live with them.'

Even so just the presence of troops and tanks on the streets would have been a surreal sight. At the time it surely must have been like walking on broken egg shells with people wondering if it was going to escalate further into open revolt. Would the troops open gunfire or even vice-versa with street fighting erupting in the centre of Glasgow? Must have been the question on everybody's lips.

For the establishment there was a fear that the forty-hour strike was a smoke screen. The Glasgow Herald declared the people involved as 'Bolsheviks,' pure and simple.

As the clock ticked away so would the tension as the protest seemed to reach its peak with the violence not worsening as one would expect if it was a revolt. Nevertheless, there was still a stand-off with some papers such as the Glasgow Herald believing the strike to have 'reached a natural death,' with no real seriousness by the majority involved.

A quiet agreement must have been reached as the strike committee advised people to go back to work on the 12th February 1919. Although a forty-hour week had not been achieved the working hours were reduced from fifty-four hours to forty-seven. This was still enough to provide enough of a benefit for workers as they were no longer expected to be by the yard or factory gates by six o'clock in the morning.

Repercussions for the twelve leaders involved in the strike led to them being charged and accused of forming a riotous mob to overawe and take possession of the Municipal buildings and the North British Station hotel in April 1919.

Five of the defendants Kirkwood, Gallacher, Shinwell, and Harry Hopkins had the additional charges of inciting a mob of '20,000 or thereby riotous and evilly dispossessed persons.'

During the Court hearing there had been stories that the real cause of the trouble had been caused by the 'hasty action of the Police. Maggie Craig in the 'When the Clyde ran red,' says 'the conclusion was irresistible, that some at any rate of the baton charges were made without any excuse or provocation.'

As it was, eight were acquitted and four found guilty. The fact that Davie Kirkwood had been knocked and been pictured laying concussed meant that the charges were dropped against him, especially as he had earned a lot of public sympathy.

James Murray, Willie Gallacher, and William McCartney were sentenced to three months prison for their involvement, whilst Manny Shinwell received a five-month sentence for his troubles.

It could be argued that the strike had been successful as it was agreed that there would be a reduction to a forty-hour week. With regards to the riot that led to the events of January 31st as 'Bloody Friday,' it was another event that shook the establishment in a short space of time. Questions too have to be made as to who made the decision to make the baton charge and if it was down to overzealous Policing why they had not been charged.

This though was another monumental event in 1919 and a message to the establishment that a new world was wanted after the war. Despite its importance in social history and how it led to the fight for better rights it quickly became a mere footnote in history just like the gunboats up the Mersey in 1911.

Lloyd George and the triple alliance

After the industrial disputes of 1910, 1911, and 1912 the major trade unions that represented the miners (Miners Federation of Great Britain, MFGB), the National Union of Railwaymen (NUR) and the National Transport Workers Federation (NTWF), felt that they had strength in unity. They believed that they would have more success in industrial disputes if each of the Unions supported each other even if the argument did not affect them directly.

In 1914 following a conference the MFGB, NUR, and NTWF drew an agreement which brought with it a joint membership of 1,350,000. Only the outbreak of world war one postponed the alliance being active as they got behind the war effort. R. Smillie President of the MFGB declared 'I want this Alliance of ours to be strong when we shall require the strength. And should the time ever come – we all hope that time will not arrive – when the strength of this organisation is tested, then this Alliance must either win or go under. I want it to be strong enough to make its influence sufficiently felt with the Government and the nation as to make action by this Alliance unnecessary. If it is felt by the nation that we are sufficiently strong, when we ask for changes in our conditions which are considered just and reasonable, it may not be necessary to declare what we know, as a general strike, of the three bodies.'

Following the recent unrests in the army and various trade disputes such as 'Red Clyde,' the Government were fearful of further industrial discontent which to them seemed to be breaking out like a bad virus.

To ensure that there were no plans to take matters further with plots of revolution, the Government kept tabs on any known political agitators namely Bolsheviks, and anyone that was prominent in the Trade Union movement. Lloyd George had even gone to the lengths of setting up an Industrial Unrest Committee to monitor the Trade Unions.

Despite knowing that the mood was volatile the Government proposed to reduce the rates of pay for railwaymen which had been agreed by ASLEF and NUR during the First World War. This of course did not go down well with the NUR members who proposed strike action. By doing so, this meant that the other triple alliance members could be called out to support their allies.

This meant a General strike which would affect the economy and business as they relied on coal and transport which would see the country grind to a halt. More worryingly the discontent within the army meant that they could not be relied if the strike led to disturbances or even worse a open revolt.

For Lloyd George there was only way to try and resolve the matter by inviting the leaders of the three unions to a meeting. The men invited to number 10 was Robert Smillie for the miners, James Henry Thomas present for the NUR, and Robert Williams for the transport workers.

It was pretty much a double bluff by Lloyd George when they met at number 10. He knew that disputes and a general atmosphere of unrest was breaking out across the country and that the Government was not strong enough to quash it.

Lloyd George also knew that the trade Union leaders could pretty much ask what they wanted. The question was whether they were happy with the possible repercussions should a full-scale revolt break out. Lloyd George acknowledged this with his opening gambit 'Gentlemen you have fashioned, in the Triple Alliance of the Unions represented by you, a most powerful instrument. I feel bound to tell you that that in our opinion we are at your mercy. The army is disaffected and cannot be relied upon. If you carry out your threat and strike, then you will defeat us.'

Carefully placing his cards, Lloyd George psychologically placed the impact of where their actions could lead them to. 'The strike will be in defiance of the government of the country and by its very success will precipitate a constitutional crisis of the first importance. For, if a force arises in the state which is stronger than the state itself, then it must be ready to take on the functions of the state or withdraw and accept the authority of the state. Gentlemen, have you considered, and if you have, are you ready?'

Lloyd George gambled correctly that the leaders of the Triple Alliance of the Unions had no intention of leading a revolution and creating mass upheaval as a result. Simon Webb the author of '1919, Britain's year of revolution,' notes 'in a very real sense, the leadership of the unions were allies of the government, and were as anxious as the Cabinet that the political system of Britain remained intact. The unions were as much a part of the establishment as the MPs at Westminster.'

Lord Northcliffe, founder of the Daily Mail, expressed his gratitude of the ruling class 'Without labour unions our strike last week would have been a civil war. It was the control of the men by their leaders which made it a peaceful struggle.'

Webb further states that this was the reason why Lloyd George did not intervene in the Glasgow strikes, lest he undermine the official trade unions. Something that Andrew Bonar Law the Chancellor of the Exchequer believed 'stating that the trade union organisation was the only thing between us and anarchy.'

As it was the railwaymen went out for nine days and won their dispute with the Government agreeing to maintain their wages for another year.

When the miners also threatened to strike in February over pay and conditions, Lloyd George set up a Royal Commission into the grievances of the striking miners. This at least put off the planned strike which in turn eliminated the threat of a General Strike as the Transport and railway workers would have come out in support.

The Sankey report was set up in March and by June 1919 the recommendation had put forward an agreement for a twenty percent increase in pay and an hour reduction of an hour in the working day. Lloyd George had gone to reject the recommendation of nationalisation and instead put forward welfare schemes to be put forward in the area.

The Triple Alliance though was to crumble two years later in April 1921 when the railwaymen and transport workers announced a decision not to go on strike to support the miners. It was cited that there was confusion over what terms the miners' union would be willing to accept. Due to this it became known as Black Friday with many socialists and trade unionists believing it to be a betrayal of the miners.

Liverpool race riots

In times of upheaval, unemployment, and uncertainty there are always those that look to outsiders and minorities to blame for their ills. Even now that is evident with the xenophobic views after the Brexit vote.

As soldiers were starting to be discharged after fighting in trenches and mud in one of the bloodiest conflicts they returned home. For their sacrifice they assumed that they would be taken care of in terms of at least being provided jobs.

That though was not forthcoming with work hard to come by and some finding that their old jobs had not been saved. Immigrants who had been brought in to keep essential work going such as the docks were brought in. Not that it was rare incidentally of immigrants finding work across the country prior to the first world war. With poverty high and no sign 'of a land fit for heroes,' there was a scapegoat that was used for the inability of getting work and that was anyone who was African or black even if they were born in Britain.

Right across the country there had been outbreaks of racist violence with Cardiff seeing four men murdered simply because of their colour. At times it was that bad that the Police and army had to be called in to restore order.

Despite Liverpool being a cosmopolitan and diverse city, it too was to suffer from hateful bigotry and racism. Liverpool had always relied on immigrants from West Africa and other parts of the globe for work there was some that believed that they had taken the work from them on the docks whilst they were fighting in the war. Although Africans and other nationalities had also fought in the war this was an inconvenient truth that was ignored by those wanting to blame someone's skin colour for their inability for finding work.

Tensions had been rising with racial insults and attacks being reported across the city. Nothing was done to try and reduce the hostility that was brewing. Inevitably the spark came when it led to serious trouble and murder that would be a tarnished part of Liverpool's history.

It came in June when John Johnson, a West Indian was in a public house enjoying a quiet drink. Two Scandinavians approached him either to intimidate or provoke John Johnson using the pretext of asking for a cigarette. When Johnson refused the Scandinavians got more hostile with a fight breaking out and ended with John Johnson being stabbed in the face.

The news quickly spread and the next evening eight of John Johnson's friends went to the pub to hunt down who was responsible for their friend's injury. Upon entering the ale house, they threw beer over those that they thought were responsible for John Johnson's attack. A fight broke out with the Police called to try and restore order. In the ensuing melee a Police Officer was knocked unconscious as it was reported that Johnson's friends escaped.

Although the Police didn't seem to make much effort in finding the assailants of John Johnson, they now sought to find the culprits who had assaulted their colleague. Upon finding the boarding house that they believed the men were holed up in, they quickly raided the premises.

It quickly turned violent as the men fought back furiously using weapons with one even using a revolver that was fired. One Policeman was shot in the mouth whilst another was hit in the neck as the fight continued. News of the event spread like a flame across a gunpowder trail as a lynch mob now used it as an excuse to storm the boarding house and mete out their own punishment.

Upon getting inside one of the inhabitants Charles Wooten a twenty-four-year-old ship fireman, who was not involved in any of the fights fled the building. This didn't deter the mob of three hundred who ran after Charles Wooten like a pack of hunting hounds with two Police Constables also in pursuit.

According to the reports the mob had chased and cornered Charles Wooten at the edge of the docks. Upon seeing their prey, the mob grabbed hold of Charles Wooten and threw him into the water. Not content with that they pelted him with rocks as he tried to swim out. Growing more tired as he was unable to get out, Charles Wooten drowned. None of the Police Officers that were present tried to stop the mob or attempted to get Charles Wooten out. Nor was one person arrested for his murder.

Despite the shocking killing it did nothing to quell the racist attacks that had been happening across the city. If anything, it increased with gangs indiscriminately attacking any black person that they could find. The Liverpool Mercury tells how a black man who held a good position with a prominent liner was hauled out of a car and robbed, whilst a black ex-serviceman who was awarded three war service medals was severely beaten up.

Another report from 10th June states how in Toxteth park, thousands of people were in a wild state of excitement. Any houses that they believed were occupied by black people were fair game to attack. Some homes were looted with one house even set on fire.

'There is a feeling of terror amongst the coloured people of the city,' wrote the Liverpool Post on its report. 'All night long until sunrise black men could be seen in companies hastening along unfrequented thoroughfares to the nearest Police station or Ethiopian Associations.'

Over time order was restored but no effort was made to bring those who had attacked someone simply because of their colour to justice. Furthermore, the mood and violence only added to the uncertainty that had come with the end of the war and the industrial unrest that had followed.

The Liverpool Police strike and another gunboat sent up the Mersey

It seems incredulous now to think that the Police would go on strike, but it was this period that ensured that no Police Officer can join a Trade Union. The dispute also had an ulterior motive for Lloyd George who wanted to make sure that the Government had full control over the Police and would not be at their mercy if they went on strike or supported other disputes. Another added incentive was to rid the ranks of those who they believed held Bolshevik sentiments.

This had all come to the fore during the last two months of the first world war when the Police went on strike in August 1918 for better pay and conditions. 'We Policemen see young van boys and slips of girls earning very much more than what we get,' said one Policeman to the Guardian 'and, well, it makes us feel very sore.'

Despite it being a sackable offence there were many Police Officers who had joined the National Union of Police and Prison Officers (NUPPO) which was formed in 1913. In its early years it operated as a secret society but with disgruntlement over wages failing to keep up with inflation, pensions, terms and conditions it made them organised and vocal.

The senior figures within the Police force decided that the best way of ending any potential trouble was to make an example of any union activity. When PC Thiel was openly vocal about fighting for better wages and conditions he was sacked. Rather than his fellow officers toeing the line they walked out in support of Thiel and to make a stand over their grievances. In London twelve thousand Police Officers had walked out when the strike had been called.

Due to the seriousness of the dispute Lloyd George had to come back from the front in France. With the country still at war the last thing that the Government needed was a breakdown in law and order especially with the troops still at the front. He agreed to their demands of reinstating PC Thiel, as well as an increase in pay but was carefully misleading in their requests for official union recognition.

Instead Lloyd George told them that 'the government cannot recognise a union for the police in wartime.' They took this to mean that a union would be in peace time rather than gaining confirmation that it would be when the war was over.

For many in the establishment it was a danger if the Police became unionised. Not only was there the fear that the Police may come out in support of other strikers if they became members of the TUC and the Labour party but might also encourage the army and navy for union recognition.

For the state to keep control it needed the Police and army at its side without worrying about their loyalty. Hence the reason why Lloyd George and his government sought to break any trade union activity.

The first roll of the dice for Lloyd George was appointing General Neville Macready as the new Commissioner of the Metropolitan Police. An army man, Macready also detested trade unions and was seen as the perfect man to get rid of any dissenters. In 1910 he had been sent to take control of the armed forces and the local police force to put down the strike in South Wales.

Lloyd George's next move was to set up the Desborough committee which was tasked into looking at the pay and working conditions of the Police force.

In June 1919 the Lord Desborough committee recommended an increase pay for all and free housing. As an afterthought but quite clearly a move to replace the union he recommended that a body similar to a staff association be set up to represent the views of Police Officers.

The Government announced that they intended to implement the recommendations by introducing the Police Act. Once this was passed then it would be a sackable offence for Police Officers to be a member of a union as well as going on strike.

However, the Government offered a sweetener to giving up their rights to join a trade union by allowing Police Officers to retire on half-pay after twenty-five years' service to add onto the increase of wages that had also been agreed.

For NUPPO it left them no choice. It was either accepting the terms but give up trade union recognition and disband. It was a case of fight or die for NUPPO. A national Police strike was therefore called for the 31st July 1919 with the hope that its members would believe that trade union recognition was a matter worth fighting for.

Although membership for NUPPO had increased quite considerably after the 1918 dispute it was the government who felt that they were in a stronger position than they were the year before. With the offer of better wages and conditions in lieu of surrendering their right to join a union and strike the Government relied on this for the majority of Police Officers to accept.

The stakes were further raised with a carrot and a stick approach as the government announced that any Police Officer going out on strike would face instant dismissal. Furthermore, all pension rights would also be forfeited. However, to get them to think the 'right way,' the Government arranged that all Police Officers would be given an advance on their increase pay, that very week, of £10 each.

The strike was a disaster. For many Police Officers they had got what they wanted in terms of better wages and conditions without the need to strike. Added to which the loss of pension rights was too much to risk and were quite happy for the proposed Police body to represent their interests.

Another success for the government wasn't just ensuring the loyalty and support of the Police but ridding them of the left-wing agitators who they felt were undermining their authority. However, there was only one city were the strike was highly supported and would cause significant problems and that was the second biggest city of the country, Liverpool.

Due to the unrest during the past year there was understandable concern about what might happen with the lack of Policemen if the strike was well supported in Liverpool. Not only that, but eight years earlier the Transport Strike had brought Liverpool to a virtual standstill and at the mercy of the strike committee. With the recent events with the mutinies that had taken place in the army, there was a fear that those with a political agenda might see this as an opportunity and use Liverpool's position as the second city to attempt a revolution.

The reasons why the Liverpool Police strike was widely supported was not due to trade union recognition, but other conditions imposed on them by the watch committee. Pay was of course on the agenda but there was resentment from the junior ranks over the strict discipline that was enforced. Every day when called for parade they were marched around like soldiers on the drill square.

Another complaint was that despite being on low pay, the watch committee insisted that they should live in the 'better off,' areas of the city. As these were expensive places to reside in, they were expected to live a middle-class lifestyle on a labourers' wage.

Like the other Police forces across the country the local watch committee on the day the strike was to commence, warned that if no Police Constable reported for parade by eight pm then they would be dismissed by the force. It was enough for some to report but more than half of the Liverpool Constables failed to show up for duty.

As word broke out that the Police were heavily depleted the mayhem started. There had been trouble previously but many saw it as an opportunity to show the authorities what they thought of them whilst taking advantage of taking goods to either sell or use. Simon Webb illustrates this in 1919 the year of revolution by saying 'it was a spontaneously outpouring of anger, with a strong business edge.'

The authorities thought that by enrolling special constables who were sworn in and issued batons would be enough to deter any would be rioters. Not surprisingly the rag tag men of shopkeepers and businessmen was not enough to stop the riots that did break out. It wasn't just lacking in numbers but training in dealing with violent crowds. At one point while a shop was being looted a special constable stood like a hapless goalkeeper as rioters swooped past him to take what they wanted from a shop.

Scotland Road, Byrom Street and Great Homer Street was where the main trouble started. Clothes shops, jewellers and pawnbrokers were the main targets as the looting spread across the city.

With no sign of the rioting and looting being contained with the broken windows and debris strewn about the street, like an invasion, the government resorted to calling in the troops. Not only that and to ensure that they meant business the super-dreadnought HMS Valiant was ordered to sail straight to Liverpool. Weighing in at 29,150 tons it was as long as London's BT tower and with its eight 15in guns, twelve 6in guns and four torpedo tubes it was a match for any ship in the world. It set sail with two destroyers heading to Liverpool after getting permission from Winston Churchill.

There was a practical side for a naval task force so that the sailors could secure the docks and protect the docks from rioters. On the second night of the disturbances the dock gates had been set on fire. However, the other reason was to show the occupants of Liverpool that the government would use any force necessary to subdue the city.

It even led to the government of sending in troops with full battle kit on. Not only that but like Glasgow earlier in the year tanks were also sent to patrol the streets of the city. It was quite a surreal sight to see soldiers and tanks roaming the street in what was meant to be peace time. There was an unreal sense of being occupied and wondering what would happen next. Would the troops open fire on civilians, would tanks be used to smash the crowds?

It was enough to quell any disturbances during the day, but trouble reared its head on Saturday night as a jewellers' window was smashed by the Rotunda theatre. An extract from Pat O'Mara 'autobiography of a Liverpool slummy' gives a vivid account of the looting.

"The bobbies were on strike! There were no bobbies! That could only mean one thing, and that thing happened. I was coming out of the Daulby Hall with Jackie Sanchez (having mooched the entrance fee from him) at the time when the first fever caught on. We went across the street to Skranvinsky's chip-and-fish shop and listened to speculations over this new and strange strike. As we stood in the crowd a couple of bucks walked in, ordered in some chips and fish and refused to pay for them, suggesting to the hysterical Mrs Skranvinsky that she "get a bloody bobby!" Then they walked out, followed by others not yet paid up, who had taken the hint. Some leaned across the counter and grabbed handfuls of chips and fish and scallops, and without waiting to salt them, continued brazenly out into the street. Only Mrs Skravinsky's screams kept those on the outside at bay."

"There were no bobbies! We were outside. On the corners here and there stood the bobbies, grimly passive and, to signify the fact, with no official labels on their arms. Excited groups of hooligans eyed them wonderingly. A jewelry window just down London Road crashed in, and as bobbies smiled wonder vanished from the hooligans. Another window crashed in. It was the Lusitania all over again (in 1915 after the passenger ship the Lusitania was sank, riots broke out in an expression of anti-German feeling) only much more intense, since now there was no restraining hand at all. Hands were out grasping through the jewelry store windows. Inside other stores whose windows were bash in, respectable-looking men and women joined with slummies to gather up loot and flee homeward. Every store with anything worth steeling was broken into and the furnishings wrecked in the frenzy to get the best stuff available. I did not have anything like good luck until Ben

Hyde's pawnshop farther down London Road was reached. After the windows were bashed in, the place was ransacked, lockers pulled out, pledged articles tucked into aprons. I got hold of a couple of muffs that struck me, in my innocence, as very expensive things and once outside, fearing the riot would be short lived, I skipped away from Jackie, tucked two precious furs under my coat, and sped along the comparatively quiet streets for home."

Soldiers were rushed to the scene as a stand-off between them and the rioters ensued. A magistrate tried to read the riot act, but this was jeered and ignored. With the crowd getting more hostile and fearing that they were going to be overwhelmed the soldiers fired warning shots over the heads of the rioters.

That may have been enough to quieten down that area, but the troops were still stretched. So much so that like the specials previously, some soldiers stood helplessly by as looters stormed a clothes shop and took their booty like a Viking raid on tour. One report mentions of men bringing a horse and cart and robbing a shop of its entire stock. In Birkenhead the riot act was read by a magistrate in an armoured car as trouble spread over the water.

Despite the special constables being effective as a cat flap in an elephant house, the mayor sent an appeal to be read out at every Sunday church service for all able-bodied men to sign up as special constables for the month.

To make matters worse a bakers' strike had begun with the tram drivers now threatening to go out for better pay and conditions. Added to which the railway men were also considering in going out to support the Police strike.

In a move that would have made the government even more twitchy and wonder if it was a secret Bolshevik plot to overthrow the state, the local branch of the Labour party passed a resolution for a general strike 'that the Liverpool Trade Unionists declare common cause with the National Association of Police and Prison Officers, and that in order to give immediate and necessary assistance a down tools be herewith declared. All trade unionists of this district are agreed to cease work at once on account of the attack made by the government on trade unionism.'

Even with the added presence of troops on the street and warships it still wasn't enough to deter the rioters who were growing increasingly bolder. On the Sunday a brewery in Love lane was looted with men getting drunk on the beer. So much so that they did not notice a truck load of soldiers who had been dispatched to restore order.

A rumour had spread that the soldiers did not have live ammunition as the crowd became more hostile even though troops fired a warning shot. This led to a man called Thomas Hewlett grabbing hold of a soldier's rifle and in the ensuing tug of war the rifle went off and fatally wounded Hewlett in the thigh as he died in hospital the following day.

Elsewhere in the city, stones were thrown at troops as matters became increasingly volatile as looting continued across the city. In one area troops fired on the crowd with one man being taken to hospital with a bullet wound to his neck.

By nightfall a large crowd started to congregate by St. George's Hall by where the tanks were stationed. Looting had begun again along London road with the soldiers firing over the rioters' heads as Police and special constables' baton charged the crowd.

Fighting between the rioters and soldiers continued with a crowd charging two soldiers by Christian street. Warning shots were fired and with a body of Police Officers on the scene they launched a baton charge that managed to drive the crowd away.

It was reaching a critical condition as rioting and looting continued that the army set up a Lewis gun in London road. This showed the nervousness and the battle for control that the authorities deemed it necessary to set up a gun that was aimed along the length of the street so that they could fire right up and down the road. No matter that rioting and looting had taken place it was a frightening and sobering thought that the authorities were willing to fire on civilians. Paranoia it seemed was haunting the government that this was the start of a revolution.

Over in Birkenhead the troops had managed to just about to secure the docks to stop any fear that any saboteurs would sabotage any machinery. Troops were even stationed around Birkenhead town hall when a rumour spread that rioters were going to burn it to the ground.

The tram strike on the Monday went ahead which caused vast disruption as the majority of workers relied on the trams to get to work. Added to which there was still the prospect of the railway workers going out on strike to support the striking Policemen. To make the government even more twitchy at whether there was an uprising on the cards the Liverpool District Vigilance Committee had been set up.

A change in tactics also saw soldiers being relieved of their full kit and rather than carrying a rifle were issued pickaxe handles. Parts of Liverpool were called off limits to prevent further trouble. However, it was to be the weather and the heavy rain that stopped people congregating that following Monday night.

It was enough to put an end to the rioting and looting as it started to fizzle out. Over four hundred people were charged with looting or rioting. With regards to the Police strike, there was a recruitment drive to replace the Police Constables who had gone on strike. Not one man was reinstated with some having to leave the city to find work. Adverts by local firms made it specifically clear that any Police Officers who were dismissed need not apply. The figures state that 955 were sacked.

Sellwood of the Police strike 1919 (printed 1978) gives a vivid picture of the former Police officers having to return their uniform which they did by piling it up outside St. George's Hall. 'The uniforms started to pile up a mass of blue/black serge often interrupted by splashes of colour. Campaign ribbon medals above the tunic's left breast pocket bore witness to the meticulous years of service given to the city and the country that the former wearers had given.'

For Lloyd George and his government, the strike had purged the Police of any unsavoury and suspected Bolshevik supporters. It also ensured that the state would always have control over the Police and even now it is illegal for a Police Officer to strike or join a trade union. There is of course a Police association where Officers can put forward their grievances, but they are not in the position to enter an industrial dispute. In short Lloyd George had ruthlessly shown his hand in curbing any further threats the Police Union NAPPO may have had.

1919 the year of near revolution

By the end of the first world war there was still the tremors of the after affects from the repercussions. Empires had fallen, maps had changed drastically, and the Russian revolution had seen the Bolshevik's overthrow Tsar Nicholas II. In Germany Kaiser Wilhelm II had been forced to abdicate.

This was a new world for Britain which was the beginning of the end of the British Empire. It was also quite worrying for the establishment that revolution may hit the shores of Britain. There had been industrial disputes prior to the war and with new political ideals that had surged through Russia it was unsettling times as these ideals were being adopted by some in Britain.

With many of these soldiers or former troops who were now experienced fighters it didn't bode well if something was ignited in Britain.

That was why the mutinies that happened in the army had caused alarm and panic. Especially when committees had been set up which had been like the mutinies in Russia as the soldiers took charge over their officers.

As the mutinies increased there was uncertainty over whether the government could trust the troops if called upon. Indeed, it must have crossed the minds of the likes of Winston Churchill as the soldiers marched up Whitehall whether the moment for revolution had come.

The Guards loyalty was crucial but equally it could quite easily have turned into a bloodbath if a gun had been fired during the standoff.

It had not helped the government over the disgruntlement within the army when Lloyd George had promised 'swift demobilisation,' and the possibility of being sent to fight in Russia. Such was the paranoia of Bolshevism there was suspicions that Lloyd George was a secret Bolshevik. This feeling came over his reluctance to pursue a war with Russia as some plotted to overthrow him. Winston Churchill incidentally was privy to these plans to remove Lloyd George.

One thing is certain and that was Lloyd George was not a Bolshevik. He was a pragmatic man who knew the limitations of a military intervention in Russia. It wasn't ideal, but it was best to make a deal in order to concentrate on Britain reasserting its authority and keeping control of its Empire. Then there was the matter of more costs that another war would bring.

Ruthlessness was also another key part of Lloyd George who pulled the rug under Winston Churchill. Whilst the latter was still obsessing over Bolshevism and Russia, Lloyd George shot down any plans that it would go further in a speech that also threw Churchill to the backwaters of the benches.

1919 was a year of unrest and with the right political drive it could quite easily have led to revolution. It had all the potential ingredients of unrest within the army, strikes and demonstrations such as in Glasgow that were heavily put down, and riots in Liverpool that saw troops, tanks, plus a gunboat being sent up the Mersey.

It would be easy to just dismiss the events of 1919 as a mere hiccup of discontent as the country slowly rebuilt itself to normality. The fact was that the world had changed. Whether the establishment was aware, but it was the beginning of the end of the British Empire. For working class people after suffering in the war they wanted a better life and were prepared to fight for it.

This didn't mean revolution and certainly not for the Trade Unionists. It was why with the triple alliance that Lloyd George was able to call the trade union leaders bluff. For them their priority was improving working conditions, hours, and wages. Running the country certainly didn't come into it.

Ironically even the trade unionist leaders were alarmed when strike committees were formed and ran by the workers as it meant that they didn't have control. More than anything it was this that probably stemmed any possible revolution occurring. However, it certainly didn't help that troops and tanks on the street gave the impression of war on the streets. In some respects, maybe it was the authorities taking no chances by ensuring that things were in place should it erupt.

The events of 1919 should be remembered as it gives an account of the mood and social changes that the end of the First World War had brought. It also shows that the country was closer to revolution than it realised.

THE CREATION OF THE NHS AND THE WELFARE STATE

Nye Bevan called the formation of the NHS 'the most civilised step any country had taken.' It was an innovation that has greatly benefitted everybody, were nobody need worry about costs for their health and receives the same high level of health care.

The formation of the NHS and the welfare state did not come easily. It came through ordinary people fighting for better rights and a decent way of living. Prior to the 5th July 1948 when the NHS was formed the lack of care and welfare was common place across the country.

Harry Leslie Smith's book 'Harry's last stand,' portrays a bleak life for the working class who were just treated as a commodity. Harry speaks of a 1930's Bradford where his Father was robbed of his pride, the poverty that his family had to endure and the helplessness when his sister Marion died of tuberculosis. As Harry said, 'you either had the dosh to pay for your medicine or you did without.' There was no NHS and Marion without medical help passed away in the workhouse infirmary.

Harry paints a vivid picture of the terraced house that he lived in as a child. 'A house that had no electricity, floors of hard slate rock sparsely covered rags coarsely woven into mats. In summer it was hot, autumn damp, and in winter bitterly cold. Spring was just like autumn in the sense it was wet.'

There was hardly any furniture whilst Harry shared a battered mattress with his older sister Alberta that hosted insects 'and reeked of time and other people's piss.' When it was cold there would be frost on the pane as they tried to stay warm.

Work was to be found down the mines for Harry's Father like many others who worked long and dangerous shifts. In some respects' life was not living but surviving.

Memories of their own struggles as Harry's Parents generations was still fresh in the memory. That was why they were determined that after the Second World War that there would be a new, fairer world. It was partly the reason why Labour won such a large majority.

Prior to Labour winning their first massive landslide the quality of healthcare for those without money was poor. For those who were unfortunate enough to be ill in the poor house then the quality of care was low and minimal at best.

A lot of the nursing care was carried out by other inmates whilst paid nursing was minimal, part-time, and poorly paid. Joseph Rogers writing about his own time as a workhouse Doctor, reported that he had no paid nurses to care for over five hundred sick inmates. If he needed to administer any medication then this would have to come out of his own pay packet of £50 a year, meaning that treating patients would affect him making a living. Consequently, it wasn't a surprise that some workhouse Doctors gave different coloured water for every ailment to avoid charges. Patients were kept in poorly ventilated areas with no washing facilities whilst contagious fever patients were spread around the hospital which meant the fever spread. Prominent figures such as Florence Nightingale described the workhouse hospitals as 'worse than those in the Crimean war.'

Due to heavy campaigning there were changes although this wasn't until towards the end of the nineteenth century after parliament had passed the Metropolitan Poor Act. It led to better nursing and trained medical staff as originally proposed by Florence Nightingale. There were also separate infirmaries to house patients.

In addition to these poor house institutions there was the setting up of hospitals that could be accessed by the entire population and not just the poor. These would be run by the local authorities (following a further act of parliament in 1929) and would mainly care for patients who had tuberculosis and smallpox. In effect these would be the foundations of NHS hospitals.

Voluntary hospitals were also other institutions that could also be accessed. These were normally funded by rich philanthropists and to gain admission would require a letter of recommendation from a hospital governor or the payment of fees. This could either be paid by relatives or by making weekly payments to a hospital contributory scheme. In effect paying insurance in case you became severely ill.

As medicine expanded, the voluntary hospitals became choosy in terms of which patients they would accept. Just like Hugh Laurie's, Gregory House MD, they would only select patients with diseases of interest or of a short-term illness to ensure a quick turnover of patients. It also became customary for the voluntary hospitals to offload their terminal patients such as those with cancer to the Poor House hospitals. Not surprisingly these were overburdened with patients.

During the 1930s and 1940s charity donations declined and during the war all hospitals had to work together to share staff and resources. As a result, it showed that a universal system could work and helped lead to Bevan's NHS act.

Access to a GP or Doctor prior to the NHS depended on how much money you could afford. Lloyd George introduced the National Insurance Act in 1911 which made health insurance compulsory for workers. GPs could provide medical services for working people but not for their families who had to pay.

However, there was still a large percentage of the population that had to pay for their medical treatment. Even for insured workers they were not covered for inpatient care if they were unfortunate enough to be in hospital. It meant that many suffered considerable hardship and worry if they had a serious illness.

This was a world that could be hard as Harry L Smith illustrates in his book when he was just seven years old. Harry talks about a rag and bone man offering him work in return for some broken boxes of cereal to take back home to his Mum and Dad. The Great Depression struck when Harry was six and he writes 'it was a desperate time for everyone, and it called for desperate measures. Lives and futures were sacrificed for a scrap of bread or a slice of mutton. My childhood ended in the first year of school, and I became an adult at seven. The man who drove the rag-and-bone cart was just one of many who I begged from to keep my Parents fed until I was able to find work as a beer barrow boy. The harsh visions from my boyhood and the poverty I have endured have haunted me through my adult life.' It was why with the growth of the Labour party it meant that ordinary people could have more of an influential say in making changes that people wanted and needed.

With victory starting to look likely for the allies that plans, and ideals were openly discussed for a better future. Britain needed re-building in terms of housing, social care, and jobs. For a lot of people there were those that still had fresh memories of what life was like after the first world war. The lack of jobs and poverty was certainly no land fit for heroes. Now there was a party who would help bring about the changes people wanted.

Plans were already being put into place for the type of reforms that would be required for a new Britain. The Beveridge report of 1942 was the blueprint of the formation of the NHS. Senior civil servant Sir William Beveridge chaired the committee who were tasked with reviewing social services schemes. It put forward a scheme of ideas to deal with the five giant evils that blighted the lives of British people; want, disease, ignorance, squalor, and idleness.

One of the proposals was of a compulsory social security scheme that would provide benefits without means testing. All working people would pay a contribution to a state fund that could be used for a comprehensive health service, the avoidance of mass unemployment, and a system of children's allowances.

The white paper 'A national health service,' was published in 1944 outlining the wartime coalition government plans for a free, unified health service. It proposed central government management and with a health minister to be responsible for running the health service.

Not surprisingly it gained huge popularity after it was released amongst the public with over 600,000 copies released. Due to the interest and a chance of real social reform once the war was over, social reform became a political topic that was debated. As the war ended with victory for the allies, all eyes turned to the future. This was a time for real change and re-building a better Britain.

For many they could remember the hardship after the first world war with high unemployment, poverty, and ill health. Once again it was ordinary people who had helped win the war who had lost loved ones or suffered from the bombings and deaths. Now was an opportunity to make real changes.

The Labour party and Aneurin Bevan campaigned vociferously for the Beveridge report to be adopted. Despite the report's popularity the Conservatives were hostile to the report and done everything to delay and obstruct it. Winston Churchill had even described Beveridge as a 'windbag,' and 'a dreamer.'

Labour led by Clement Atlee saw this as an opportunity to seize the initiative and make bold plans that would benefit the country. A chance to make changes for the working people that they represented.

After the war in Europe had ended, a general election was called two months later. With Winston Churchill seen as a war hero who had helped Britain through its darkest hour, the Conservatives campaigned solely on the personality of Churchill.

In many respects it was a negative campaign with Winston Churchill declaring 'that the introduction of Socialism into Britain, would require some form of Gestapo, no doubt very humanely directed in the first instance.' Rather than trying to portray Churchill as a man who was equally at home as peace leader they relied solely on his record as Prime Minister during the war. Nor was there anything that attracted the war weary public of positive changes in terms of housing, jobs, nationalisation, economic reform and much needed social reforms.

Labour in contrast ran a positive campaign with its slogan Let us face the future.' It spoke of not returning to the depression of the 1930s of unemployment, inadequate health and social care. They spoke of new housing, universal health care that was based on need and not on wealth and creating jobs. Not only that but there was a high interest in politics and wanting change. The Ragged Trousered Philanthropist by Robert Tressell had become a popular read during the latter stages of the war with copies being left around after the reader had finished for it to be passed around.

There was also the other factor that Labour a party formed by trade unions and workers were in a strong position in terms of resources and experience. Several Labour MPs including the leader Clement Attlee (who had served as Deputy Prime Minister), Ernest Bevin (Minister of Labour and National Service) and Herbert Morrison (Home Secretary) had served in the war cabinet. Although it may have been in uncertain times it gave them the understanding and workings of being in government.

All these factors, plus a positive and a well-drafted manifesto that was attractive to the population put Labour on course to win the election in July 1945. Despite these factors it was the Conservatives who were favourites to claim a majority. Most political experts thought that Churchill's personality and strong leadership during the war would be enough for the public to vote for a Conservative government.

It didn't need hindsight to see that Labour was on course to win the election. The high unemployment of the 1930s was still fresh in the memories and those serving in the armed forces were aware of the bleak situation that faced the demobbed soldiers from the First World War. Labour on the other hand had an assertive manifesto to build a new and better Britain which won a lot of support. With the country needing re-building, Labour seemed to be able to provide this.

Nevertheless, it came as a huge surprise when Labour won a landslide victory with a 10.7 swing from the Conservatives to the Labour party. The largest ever achieved in a British general election. Once the results came in on the 25th July 1945, Labour had won 393 seats and the Conservatives 187. Churchill had led his party to one of its worst defeats in history.

What also needs remembering is that Churchill was not a popular figure as believed. In working class areas of Wales, Liverpool, and Yorkshire they still remembered his time as Home Secretary prior to the First World War when he sent in troops and gunboats against strikers. Some might have admired Churchill for his leadership during the war and felt his personality was what was needed for victory, but many did not see him as a leader for peacetime.

Labour didn't waste any time in using the mandate given by the voters in putting forward their ambitious manifesto. In many ways Clement Atlee's government laid the foundations of the social improvements of what modern society is used to. Even back then the changes implemented by Labour had a positive impact for the country.

Some of the policies would have been implemented by the Conservatives simply because of economic necessity. For example, the nationalisation of the coal mines would have been required simply to ensure that the industry and homes got the power that was required. The Conservatives too had plans for a national health service, but it would have been a pale imitation of Nye Bevan's NHS.

Following the Beveridge report a white paper 'a national health service,' was published in 1944 outlining the coalition government's proposals for a free universal health service. After Labour's landslide victory Aneurin Bevan was appointed the minister of health. His proposals went further than what was discussed, and, in many respects, Bevan was the architect of the NHS.

In keeping with Labour's commitment to public ownership, Bevan wanted nationalisation of municipal and voluntary hospitals with funding to come from taxation rather than National Insurance. This was a shrewd plan by Bevan, as it meant the control of the hospitals would not be insular.

After the National Health Service Act received the Royal assent in 1946, Labour moved quickly to implement the new NHS service as swiftly as possible. The major challenge was integrating these institutions into a single system. Bevan believed that full nationalisation was the only option but was acutely aware of what worked and didn't over the past century of poor relief and social insurance provision. He concluded that a system controlled by Whitehall would not work. Bevan's was a more complex system in which local health authorities, regional institutions and contractors reported back to the Ministry of Health

The NHS was planned as a three-tier structure with the Minister of Health overseeing it at the top. All three tiers would interact with each other to suit the needs of the patient. Both the municipal and voluntary hospitals were nationalised and organised into fourteen regional groups, or hospital boards.

Primary care such as GPs, dentists, opticians, all remained as self-employed professionals who were contracted by the local executive councils to provide services to the NHS so that the patient did not have to pay directly.

Lastly, there was the Local Authority Services that provided community services such as the provision of midwifery, health visits, school medical services, ambulance services, which remained the responsibility of the local authorities.

The Conservatives were satisfied with much of what Labour had proposed but they argued that too much power and responsibility was taken away from the local authorities. As a result of this they voted against the National Service Health Service Act on its second and third readings. It was to lead to negative public perceptions of the Conservatives opinion of free and universal health care.

Despite the overwhelming enthusiasm and support for a National Health Service from the public there was stiff resistance from the Doctors. Many were opposed to becoming employees of the state and felt that it would impact the money that they could make from private work. They also felt it restricted Doctors in terms of choosing patients and career. Such was the hostility that some Doctors compared Bevan's proposals to 'Nazi Germany.'

The British Medical Association even took to balloting their members to gauge their opinions. Almost ninety percent voted against the government's proposals.

Bevan remained undeterred and informed the Doctors he would cut their capitation fees which was the money that they received for each insured patient that they treated. He also prepared a motion in the House of Commons to demonstrate that Labour had a democratic mandate.

However, Bevan knew that he had to make some compromises in order to make it work. GP surgeries remained private which could be bought and sold, and the NHS effectively gave the practices contracts to provide health care. Hospital Consultants would be on a salary wage but could continue to do private work within NHS hospitals. Bevan was reported as 'stuffing their mouths full of gold,' but although he wasn't happy, he realised that there had to be some concessions.

It meant that Bevan and the BMA had managed to make a compromise with all those involved with the setting up of the NHS determined to make it work and, on the 5th July 1948, medical care became free for all people including foreigners temporally living in Britain.

Nye Bevan proudly declared on the first day that 'it was a milestone in history – the most civilised step any country had taken.' He also gave an emotional speech on the eve of the NHS launch in Manchester of the poverty that he had endured and seen in South Wales. 'First class people,' Bevan cried 'had been condemned to semi-starvation.' He recalled on how he had been forced to spending periods living off his sister's meagre wages.' Bevan spoke how he had contemplated emigrating and leaving everybody behind that he knew and loved. He knew who was to blame for this distressing situation and in words that his colleagues thought were regrettable Bevan spoke of 'a burning hatred for the Tory party that inflicted these bitter experiences on me.' The Tories 'were lower than vermin.' On Monday 5th July 1948 he hoped that his own experiences would be a thing of the past and that things would finally change for the good.

Demand for the new NHS exceeded all predictions. The number of patients rose to thirty million on Doctor's registers as people took the opportunity of free universal health care. It was an instant success with the poor being able to gain access to Doctors and medical care without the need of worrying of how they could pay. The middle classes also made full use of the NHS and so began the bold claim of ensuring free health care from 'the cradle to the grave.'

However, the costs had also exceeded expectations which caused the new government problems. During the planning of the NHS, the estimated annual cost was £170 million. In its full year of operation, the cost had risen to £305 million.

Commentators in the BMJ predicted that if the rate of expenditure continued for the NHS then it would lead to national ruin. They cited that the predicted NHS budgets had ignored the effects of an ageing population. Added to which they were dealing with more complex and expensive diseases than previously expected.

In 1950 the Chancellor Hugh Gaitskell proposed savings of £13 million by imposing charges for dentures and spectacles provided by the NHS. Nye Bevan resigned along with Harold Wilson in protest at the charges citing that this went against the free universal health care that Labour had been entrusted to provide.

Due to the heavy costs of the war, Britain's economy was in a precarious situation which put pressure on the Labour administration. At one point there was pressure on Attlee to step down, with the Conservatives claiming that Labour had no alternative but to step back from the ambitious social reconstruction that they had promised the public in 1945.

Clement Attlee remained undeterred. He conceded that reconstruction would need to feature austerity, but Britain was going to get what it voted for, not only because it was right, but contrary to what the Conservatives claimed it was financially achievable. Stafford Cripps who had been appointed chancellor in 1947 helped fashion a Keynesian approach to the economy. Taxes were kept high, particularly on undisclosed incomes such as inheritances, with estates over £21,500 subject to a 75% levy.

A deal was done with the TUC to keep wages down so that a lid could be kept on inflation. There were bumps in the road such as the devaluation crisis in 1949, but the Americans commitment of $12 billion to rebuild Europe's economy (in part to thwart the threat of communism) through the Marshall plan helped Labour steady the ship.

Cripps was to keep a tight rein with regards to the budget over re-housing by implementing spending cuts. It hit plans to build five million new homes within a decade. This was to have repercussions with 38,000 evacuees still waiting to be re-housed in March 1946. Added to which the government channelled a lot of money in repairing damaged housing.

Nevertheless, Labour was still serious about the problem of providing adequate working class housing which prior to the war had been poor, and had gone unsolved during the private housing boom of the 1930s.

Nye Bevan was not to be deterred from his commitment to building better working-class homes. He spent his childhood and youth in the Sirhowy Valley where his Father and himself had worked down the mines. Life had been tough for Bevan with four of his nine siblings not making it to adulthood. Bevan's own Father had died from pneumoconiosis, a lung disease contracted from the dust of working underground.

For Bevan, people like his Father had not only built Britain but had fought for it twice within the space of thirty years. The least the country could do was ensure a decent health service, and houses that had indoor toilets and were large enough for families to sit together.

To get this off the ground, local authority house-building projects were prioritised, and Bevan insisted on mixed communities where different social classes were expected to rub shoulders. The Town and Country Planning Act of 1947 planned for new substantial towns in places such as Crawley, Basildon, Harlow, and Stevenage.

Progress was slow due to so many different departments and organisations that had the ability to defer or block decisions. Cripps also kept a tight hold of finances which came under more pressure when Bevan insisted that the basic size requirements for houses were increased from 750 to 900 square feet, simply because he felt people were entitled to something better than the existing standards.

More than 195,000 houses were completed each year from 1949-51 in addition to the 227,000 that were completed in 1948. An impressive feat but still fell short of the country's needs. However, the task of building new homes was to have a positive impact over the following years. The slums of yesteryear were to be banished to history with many homes having indoor toilets and were more than fit enough to reside in.

In 1948 millions of copies of the family guide to the national insurance scheme were posted to homes up and down the country in preparation of the launch date of the 5th July 1948. The small thirty-two-page booklet informed people about the basics of the scheme they were all going to be enrolled in. From how everyone would be making contributions to how one could go and claim benefits when they needed them.

This was an ambitious, huge and complicated task with everyone working hard to ensure that it would work. Overnight the local authorities had been handed a wide range of responsibilities from planning for new housing development and education with the school leaving age raised to fifteen.

The Children Act of 1948 also made it clear that the local authorities were responsible for deprived children who either had no Parents or were unable to care for them. It led to a new approach of better relations were children were thought of as individuals and not a large mass.

Due to the National Assistant Act of 1948 the Poor laws and the Workhouses were to be finally banished with something more humane that assisted those who needed its help.

It was a momentous occasion as it saw a huge upheaval in terms of providing a better standard of living for all. There were those that were critical, who cited the problems of red tape and resentment of paying benefits to others with sneers that it was encouraging a 'Santa Claus,' state.

Some like Michael Young, director of Labour's research department and author of the party manifesto 'Let's face the future together,' thought the Welfare system was not what it could have been.

Young cited that politician didn't pay attention to the power what they had and as a result paid little attention to the damage that may be caused in the process. Instead ordinary people should have more of a say and a chance to participate in the process of change, rather than simply except what was given to them.

In 1957 Young in his book 'Family and kinship in the East London,' he acknowledged that the welfare state had brought about significant improvements but that the state disregarded things that were valuable to ordinary people. As an example, he pointed out that the effort to move working class people out of the slums to new towns and estates showed scant regards for the communities that were broken up as a result.

Nevertheless, the NHS and the welfare system introduced by the 1945 Labour government brought about significant change that overnight had a positive effect on people. In Chris Renwick's book 'Bread for all,' he gives an example of a fifty-year-old woman, a metal polisher who declared that it was 'one of the finest things that ever happened in this country.' 'In the past there's many a man had to think twice before seeing a Doctor even if he was very ill,' she explained. 'There are old people who went about for years half blind because they couldn't afford spectacles. I've seen them using bits of magnifying glass to read newspapers with and buying cheap, 2-shilling glasses which spoilt their eyes more than ever. The NHS was a godsend for people like them.'

It took a good few years for the full impact for Attlee's government's vision of what it wanted to provide to people. The post-war years saw a vast improvement in people's health and living conditions. From vaccinations, health advice, and easy access to medical and dental care to name a few, it has led to a society that up to now has provided a safety net and access to health care. There have been struggles and dangers that even now hover over the NHS and welfare system but the vision of men like Bevan have ensured that there is care for those that need it.

Comparing the life expectancies between 1948 and now 2018 emphasis this. For example, the average life expectancy for men in 1948 was 66 and women, 71. Today, men can expect to live to the age of 79.2 and women 82.9. In, terms of infant mortality in 1948 there were 34.5 deaths per 1000 live births. Today that figure is 3.7 and shows the success of the NHS and welfare system introduced by the Attlee administration.

Harry Leslie Smith in his book 'Harry's last stand,' before he passed away gives thanks to the social welfare state 'I was able to live long and see my children prosper,' Harry writes about the fight to protect the NHS and welfare state. The book gives a vivid account of what life was like prior to the welfare state and of the poverty that people endured. In his concluding chapter Harry declares that 'in the 1940s, 1950s, and 1960s we treated poverty and social inequalities like we treated polio and other infectious diseases; a threat to mankind.' Harry adds 'For over a generation, British society worked together for one common aim: measured prosperity for everyone. To achieve it, free health care and education were provided to every citizen to even out the playing field of life. Its motives was both idealistic and practical, because in the end it permitted Britain to compete economically in the industrialised twentieth century market place.'

Undoubtedly the introduction of the welfare state and NHS as had such a massive impact on our lives today. None of it came easy, with every inch fought for. However, the end of the second world war there was a determination not just to rebuild the country but one that future generations would benefit and not have to suffer the ill health and terrible conditions that they and their families had to endure previously. As a result, the policies of the 1945 Labour government with men such as Bevan have helped shaped and better our world.

DIXIE DEAN – FOOTBALL'S FIRST NUMBER 9

GERD MÜLLER called Lionel Messi an "incredible player" after the Argentine broke his record of 85 goals in a calendar year. Much was made of the records broken by Messi as he went on to score a record-breaking 50 La Liga goals in the 2011-12 season. Nothing, however, was mentioned of a footballer who, in his day, was as big as Messi and scored goals with just as much ease.

In one season he scored a record-breaking 60 league goals. Such was his fame that the baseball icon Babe Ruth wanted to meet his sporting tantamount. The man in question was William 'Dixie' Dean.

It is a remarkable story that has all the twists and drama of a Hollywood film: from Dean nearly losing his life and being told that he would never walk again, to producing a dramatic finale a season later that would propel Everton to winning the league and breaking a goal scoring record that still stands today.

Sir Matt Busby had this to say of playing against his Evertonian rival: "To play against Dixie Dean was at once a delight and a nightmare. He was a perfect specimen of an athlete, beautifully proportioned, with immense strength, adept on the ground but with extraordinary skill in the air."

It was Tranmere Rovers who first signed Dixie Dean, a man born in nearby Birkenhead. His ability quickly drew the interest of much bigger clubs – including Arsenal and Newcastle – however it was Everton's £3,000 bid that was accepted, with an excited Dean running the two and half miles to the Woodside hotel to agree the contract.

There was an initial sour taste to the deal as Dean believed that a £300 payment, agreed to be given to his parents, only turned out to be £30. Dean appealed but was told by a league official, "I'm afraid you've signed and that's it."

Though his signing bonus failed to live up to expectation, the same wasn't the case for Dean himself. He was good in the air, strong off either foot, and electric over the ground. There is scarcely any footage of Dean but in one of the few clips available on the internet, it shows Dean scoring with a powerful header. It is the intense concentration and movement, even in those few seconds, that makes you realise Dean does indeed belong to those elite players over the eras.

It is the ability to see things five steps quicker and to anticipate when to make your move; to know when to shoot or to pass to a teammate who is in a much better position to score. Busby had this to say of Dean's footballing brain: "He was incredibly unselfish and an amazingly accurate layer-off of chances for others."

A clip of Dean in the now-legendary 1933 FA Cup final shows his lithe movement and ability to read the game that bit quicker. All it takes is a loose ball, with Dean swiftly taking the advantage before laying it onto a teammate. It is that bit of skill that will remain timeless and ultimately sought after by up and coming strikers.

No matter what the era is, you can guarantee that the opposition will try to physically stop you. Part of the game is having the mental strength and awareness, such as **George Best** avoiding Chelsea's Ron 'Chopper' Harris, to evade the defender and score.

Dean too was kicked hard but was perfectly capable of looking after himself, something the media at the time noted and praised him for. In a match against Altrincham, when playing for Tranmere, Dean received such a vicious tackle that he ended up losing a testicle. Reports at the time quoted Dean as advising a team-mate not to rub the affected area: "Don't rub 'em, count em!"

In Dean's first full season for Everton he scored 32 goals in 38 appearances; it instantly elevated him to fans' favourite status. However, Dean was meant to have disliked the nickname 'Dixie' – it referred to his hair and dark complexion, like that of someone being from the southern parts of the United States.

Tragedy was to strike in the summer of 1926 when Dean, taking his girlfriend out on his motorcycle in Wales, collided with another bike. Dean's injuries were so serious that at one point doctors thought he would die. Even after overcoming his life-threatening injuries, Dean was told to forget about football and to come to terms with the fact that he might never walk again.

To the astonishment of the medical staff, Dean made a full recovery and was able to start training with Everton again. Indeed, upon returning back to the squad in October 1926 Dean scored 21 goals in just 27 appearances.

Such was Dean's prowess in the air that hilarious rumours abound that the metal plate installed in his skull after his accident was the reason for Dean's ability and power in the air. The plate had actually been removed prior to Dean returning to football, although it didn't stop the story circulating. The rumours that engulf the game had an early start.

A true footballing great became a legend for his side with his presence raising morale, not just amongst the support but team-mates as well. With Dean back in the team it made Everton believe that anything was possible. The Englishman was someone they could turn to and would deliver when required. It's the ultimate sign of a legend.

It was the 1927-28 season that was to be the pinnacle of Dean's career as he scored a record-breaking 60 league goals – which helped Everton to clinch the title. Huddersfield led the table, with Everton trailing the Yorkshire side by four points in the mid-March, boasting a game in hand over their Merseyside rivals, too.

Everton, though, demonstrated the mentality which is needed to win a league championship by embarking on an eight-game unbeaten run, winning six and drawing two. It was Dean's two goals in a 4-2 win against Blackburn – on April 6 – that was seen as driving much-needed pressure to Huddersfield. The Toffees were now just one point behind.

All top strikers need a strong and focused mentality, especially under pressure. With Everton putting the squeeze on a faltering Huddersfield, it's the big players, like Dean, that team-mates and supporters rely upon. The expectation of scoring, especially with all the talk of breaking Middlesbrough legend George Camsell's record, must have weighed heavy on the broad shoulders of Dean.

Huddersfield, despite having games in hand, wilted under the pressure, and by April's end they were three points behind Everton – who only needed a point to be champions. As it was, Huddersfield couldn't even push their rivals as they lost 3-0 away to Aston Villa. Everton were now officially the First Division champions.

There was still plenty of drama, with talk in the terraces and papers surrounding whether Dean would break Camsell's record of 59 league goals, set in the previous campaign as *Boro* clinched promotion to the First Division. With only three games left Dean stood at 51 goals, nine shy of the record.

If there was one thing guaranteed with Dean, it was that win or lose, he would provide a spectacle with his shooting ability, power and touch. Two goals against Aston Villa in a 3-2 win for Everton and four against Burnley, as the Toffee's won 5-3 away, brought him close to the record. It meant that a hat-trick was required in the final home against Arsenal. Sixty-thousand fans saw Dean score within the first five minutes; later on in the first half Everton were awarded a penalty which Dean dispatched with classic confidence.

With just eight minutes remaining, the crowd looked on anxiously as Troupe crossed into the box. The unflappable Dean, waiting for his chance to break a record that many thought was unbreakable, attacked the ball and headed in. Not even an Arsenal equaliser could dampen the spirits inside Goodison. The crowd that day was lucky to witness the very best of England's first world-class goal-scorer.

Thanks to Dean's record-breaking season he was now something of a celebrity. He was even paid to endorse Wix cigarettes with the line 'England's greatest goal-scorer declaring the taste to be excellent'.

Offers also came to play football in the States with Arsenal's **Herbert Chapman** also putting in a bid. Although Dean stated he had no desire to leave Everton it wasn't really in his hands even if he had wanted to. After all, this was an era where the clubs had ultimate control over when and where a player would go.

Over the next two years Everton suffered a blip and the ignominy of relegation in 1930. The team came straight back up and, in their return to the top flight, won the 1932 league title – with Dean scoring 45 goals in just 38 appearances.

Although not as dramatic as the 1927-28 season, there was a controversial incident that added to the folklore of Dean. In 1932, an end of season tour was arranged in Nazi Germany. Prior to the six games, the Everton team was told that they would be required to do the Nazi salute before kick-off. Dean and his team-mates reacted furiously to the request. Led by their talisman, the players informed the officials that they were not going to do the Nazi salute, despite political pressure. Furthermore the players were incensed with the derogatory and racist cartoons about Dean's appearance circulating before the matches.

This refusal caused unbridled controversy, with the Nazi's viewing it as a direct snub. From a propaganda perspective the salute from Everton, who were viewed as a major footballing heavyweight, and from one of the world's greats like Dean, would have given the Nazis respectability across the world stage. It was this snub that led to intense pressure when England and Aston Villa later toured Germany in 1938. With the political position far more volatile than in 1932 – the fear that the slightest spark could start war – both teams were told to perform the Nazi salute.

Aston Villa refused in their first two games but succumbed to the pressure in their third game, although the players did stick two fingers up after conducting the salute. England, of course, did perform the infamous salute, but such was the pressure from the Football Association and political bodies that the slightest issue could start another war, they ultimately felt forced to do so.

The following year Dean officially became the first number 9 as he lifted the FA Cup for Everton after they overcome Manchester City in the final. It was the first game that numbers were printed on the back of players' shirts, with Everton 1-11 and City 12-22.

Injuries were starting to catch up with Dean and in the brutal world of football there was no sentiment. This was something that Dean seemed to understand himself when a young Tommy Lawton was introduced to the Everton changing room after a match. "Youngster," said Dean, "You've come here to take my place. Anything that I can do to help you, I will."

Even so, the Everton board failed to show their gratitude to one of their sporting icons; a man adored by the Goodison faithful. As with all clubs of that era – and for years onwards – players were seen as commodities, to be used and discarded at will. In effect, Dean was more or less left to clear his locker quietly after a deal had been agreed for him to join Notts County in 1937. It took Everton until 1964 to arrange a testimonial for Dean, with an England vs. Scotland game consisting of players from Everton and Liverpool.

Although Dean had only scored three goals in nine appearances for *The Magpies*, he still had the draw of being a star when he signed for Sligo in

January 1939. A huge crowd waited at the train station to see their new hero, while a later move to Hurst FC (now Ashton) in the Cheshire league earned the club £140 in his final game.

For whatever reason, Dean only earned 16 caps for England despite scoring 18 goals in those appearances. There are stories that Dean was openly critical of the FA selection board but there is no evidence to confirm this.

After finishing his career in football Dean followed the time-honoured tradition of running a pub, the Dublin Packer in Chester. He later became a porter at Littlewoods with the job arranged by Everton chairman Sir John Moores.

In Dean's later years he became seriously ill with influenza and had to be admitted to hospital in 1972. Four years later, following a blood clot, Dean had to have his right leg amputated. Sadly, it forced much of his time to be spent indoors. Despite ill-health Dean attended Goodison Park to watch his beloved Everton play Liverpool in the 1980 Merseyside derby, but suffered a heart attack whilst watching the game and tragically passed away aged 73.

Bill Shankly, legendary manager and famous rival of Everton, had this to say of Dean at his funeral: "Ladies and gentlemen, today we are joined by a man who ranks amongst the greatest there is, Shakespeare, Rembrandt and Bach, this man is Dixie Dean."

The goal-scoring statistics of Dean are phenomenal. At Everton he bagged 349 league goals in 399 appearances, whilst also scoring 37 hat-tricks. On average, it equated to 0.94 goals per game. In the FA Cup his 32 appearances saw Dean score 28 goals. In modern terms, there remains one record that Messi has yet to match: Dean's 60 league goals in a season.

His talent was ahead of his time, and his records still stand long after his death. William 'Dixie' Dean: football's first great number 9.

JOE FAGAN – THE QUIET CHAMPION

THE DEMEANOUR AND ACTIONS OF JOE FAGAN were of a modest man who would give his time to anyone. No job was beneath him, and to have passed him in the street as he made the short walk from his house to Anfield you might not have looked twice.

However, he was no Ordinary Joe; he contributed to the success that Liverpool enjoyed throughout the 1970s and '80s like few others. Not only did Fagan help **Bill Shankly** and Bob Paisley re-build Liverpool from scratch, he also managed Liverpool to their most successful season ever by claiming a treble.

Achievements like these would normally guarantee you a place amongst the pantheon of football greats. Winning a league championship over a marathon season, a League Cup when it was taken just as seriously as the FA Cup, and beating a Roma side in the European Cup final in their own backyard is the stuff of legend. Even the following season, which would be his final year as manager, saw Fagan guide Liverpool to a runners-up spot in the league and a European Cup final.

Joe Fagan, however, would never have liked to have been referred to as a legend. He was a man who didn't seek any platitudes or boast an ego. Instead, Fagan was happy to get on with his job and live his life through his love for football.

There are some critics who will try to state that the team that Fagan inherited was still in its prime and just needed a steady hand to keep things ticking over. This, though, is not only ignorant but sloppily glosses over the talents of a man who was more than just a top coach. As David Moyes, Wilf McGuinness and Brian Clough found out to their cost, it is hard to follow after one legend, never mind two, which was the case with Fagan.

For the Liverpool board, appointing Fagan seemed a relatively easy decision to make after Bob Paisley had announced his wished to retire from football after the 1982-83 season. After all, Joe Fagan was an original member of the famed Boot Room. He was just as responsible for the evolving changes in tactics as well as being liked and respected by fellow coaches, players and supporters.

The job was something that Fagan wasn't too sure about at the time: "My first reaction at the time was that I wouldn't take it, but I thought about it carefully and realised someone else might come in and upset the whole rhythm. I finally decided to take it and keep the continuity going for a little longer."

At 62, Fagan was one of the oldest managers in the league and was only a couple of years younger than Paisley.

Despite being born in Liverpool, he started his career as a defender for Manchester City, and although there was little success, he did captain the team. After that there were early coaching stints as player-manager at Nelson and assistant manager at Rochdale, before taking up the offer of a coaching role at Liverpool by the then-manager Phil Taylor.

With the departure of Taylor after Liverpool failed to gain promotion, there was, of course, much uncertainty whether new manager Bill Shankly would bring in his own staff. It was to be one of the best decisions that Shankly made as he enforced no changes to the coaching set up. Indeed, his first words to Fagan were: "You must have been a good player, Joe, because I tried to sign you."

The foundations of Shankly's Liverpool were helped by Paisley, Fagan, Moran, Bennett and Saunders, who helped turn a dilapidated club with poor training facilities kicking and screaming into a first-rate club that became the "bastion of invincibility" that Shankly wanted.

Although Fagan had been given the job as reserve team manager, he was still to have an influential part to play in helping establishing Liverpool as a major force. No job was seen to be beneath anyone, with all expected to muck in for the common good. Whether it was helping clear rocks from the battered Melwood training pitch and making it a surface suitable for a top club, or painting the barriers at Anfield, Fagan, like Paisley and Shankly, was always willing to pitch in.

Part of the success of Liverpool was that nobody was allowed to get any airs or graces. Shankly, Paisley and Fagan were from a generation rife with poverty and, as soon as they were old enough, were expected to graft and earn for the family. It was a philosophy that influenced their outlook on life, and if a player wasn't giving their all then they were shown the door.

Tommy Smith recalls the time that Fagan would not allow for any illusions of grandeur. After two years on the ground staff, Smith had been offered a professional contract. Prior to signing the contract, his ground staff colleagues asked if he would help sweep the home dressing room in order to finish quickly. Smith scoffed at such a suggestion now that he was to be a professional and let them know that his days of skivvying were behind him.

Unbeknown to Smith, Fagan had been watching all of this in the background and, with the sigh of an uncle telling off a petulant nephew, said: "Tommy, pick up the brush, son." No more needed to be said as an embarrassed Smith picked up the brush and helped his friends.

One of Fagan's strengths was his ability to listen to players and offer advice when needed. Roger Hunt had signed amateur terms whilst doing his national service, which in turn restricted him playing. As a result, Hunt found himself struggling with his fitness – so much so that after being selected to play against Preston for the reserves, his performance deteriorated so badly that midway through the second half Fagan pushed his captain John Nicholson up front with Hunt dropping back in defence.

It's what was said after the game that even now sticks in Hunt's mind. Fagan quietly told him that he was not attempting to make a show of him but advised him what he needed to do if Hunt wanted to make it as a professional footballer. Hunt recalls: "I decided to get even fitter, work harder, and at least if I didn't make it at least I had given it everything. I always remember that part of it because Joe was solely responsible." The advice worked: Hunt became a Liverpool legend.

One of the most difficult tasks of being a reserve team manager is how to deal with the senior professionals who have been dropped from the first team. After the defeat against Watford in a third round FA Cup tie, Shankly had realised that the team needed rebuilding and that he had perhaps allowed players to stay past their prime.

Ian St. John was one of the senior pros to be part of the cull and Fagan was aware that he had to ensure that not only would St. John do his best on the pitch, but not cause disruption like many a disgruntled former first teamer does in football.

Man management was one of Fagan's strengths as he ensured that he would ask St. John's opinion in front of his team-mates, as well as making him captain. Through Fagan's tactful diplomacy he made what was a rough part of

St. John's career smoother, as well as ensuring that he also performed on the pitch, even if it was only for the second string.

With up and coming youngsters who were impatient at wanting to get in the first team like Ray Clemence, Brian Hall, Tommy Smith and Ian Callaghan, Fagan would show the patience and tutoring required that would help these players make the step up. Brian Hall said about his time under Fagan: "His thinking was always football-orientated, but above that he was a real people's person."

The reserves only lost 14 of their 126 Central League fixtures under Fagan, and it resulted in three consecutive championships between 1969 and 1971.

Fagan, like all good managers, wasn't averse to laying down the law verbally. Graeme Souness recalled some years later: "His way would be a quiet word or even a single look. He could be hard and I remember on a number of occasions that he would say something really harsh to one of the lads, but he'd do it ever so quietly and that was his way of emphasising the point."

Fagan knew when it was appropriate to put an arm around a player, to offer practical advice, and when to lay into them. Mark Lawrenson recalls that a telling off from Joe Fagan felt like the end of the world: "It [Fagan's shouting] had a far bigger effect than anyone else at the club doing it – even Bob Paisley or Kenny Dalglish afterwards."

In many ways Shankly, Paisley and Fagan were a holy trinity with their own individual skills and talents coming together to help make Liverpool so successful. The fabled Boot Room is now talked about in mythical terms. It was, as the name suggests, where the boots were kept but became a base for the backroom staff and manager to have a chat about the football or issues affecting the club.

Fagan indirectly was responsible for creating it all. As a favour to his friend Paul Orr, who was then manager of local amateur side Guinness Exports, Fagan would do a spot of coaching and arranged for injured Export players to be treated at Anfield. As a thank you, Orr would regularly send supplies of Guinness and other ales for Fagan.

The only problem was where to store it, with Fagan finding that the Boot Room was a handy place. With a ready supply of ale, it became the go-to place for the coaching staff to meet. Bob Paisley once commented: "It's just like popping down the local. We have a full and frank exchange of views in there in a leisurely atmosphere every Sunday morning."

Shankly might have been quoted as saying that "football is a simple game based on the giving and receiving of passes" – a view that Paisley and Joe Fagan also shared – but that underplayed the hard work and thought that went into their preparations.

When Shankly took over at Liverpool he instantly changed the training philosophy, which was originally geared towards physical endurance. In some quarters the lack of work with the ball made coaches believe that it made the players hungrier come Saturday.

The new regime wanted training to replicate a match, which meant working with the football. "Pass and move" became the mantra. Everything was geared towards improving technique and control, and reacting quickly to what would happen during a match. Three, four, and five-a-side matches became common, with players becoming more involved with the ball in tighter situations.

Whereas Shankly as manager would have to take a step back, Fagan was involved where he enjoyed it the most, which was working with the players. Like Paisley and Bennett, Fagan would report back to Shankly if there was anything of note from training.

Fagan, like the other coaches, was also responsible in meticulously logging each day's schedule. It was done so that in times of trouble it would be something that the coaching staff could refer to for solutions. These books were also referred to as the 'Anfield Bibles', so-called as they were meant to contain the secrets to Liverpool's success.

It was also in the Boot Room that Liverpool would discuss players and tactics. Lessons would be learnt from key games such as the the 'Mist Game' against Ajax in 1965 ,and Red Star Belgrade in 1973, which saw Liverpool change their philosophy to a more refined, passing style. The likes of Emlyn Hughes and Phil Thompson, who were good on the ball, were drafted in to play this new style, which would take them to unprecedented heights.

In 1979 Joe Fagan officially became the assistant manager. He had helped Paisley to steady the ship and take Liverpool to even greater heights after the shock resignation of Shankly in 1974.

So when Paisley announced that he would retire after the 1982-83 season, it wasn't really a surprise that Fagan would take charge; it seemed a natural transition. Fagan had the respect of the players and it was a case of business as usual. For the man himself, there was a slight difference that *he* now had to take a step back. However, any worries that he wasn't up to the task of making the tough decisions were quickly put to bed.

A pre-season tour to Belfast and Rotterdam meant Fagan had to select a 14-man squad. With Alan Hansen and Mark Lawrenson now the established centre-backs and Gary Gillispie becoming Fagan's first signing, it meant no place for the respected veteran Phil Thompson. Fagan admitted that it was his first unpleasant decision but did it because it was in the best interests of the team.

For the start of the 1983-84 season there were understandably nerves as Fagan worried that the season might be similar to Bob Paisley's first year when Liverpool finished trophyless. There were injury worries too, with Ronnie Whelan's sidelining for the beginning of the season compounded by the failure to capture Michael Laudrup and Charlie Nicholas.

It was to become a memorable season as Liverpool won a historic treble. With the Reds chasing a third successive title, the stakes were especially high as the media mused that the Reds' dominance might be on the wane.

Fagan kept a positive air with no indication of any worries or concerns about the up and coming season. It was to be justified after Liverpool thrashed Luton Town 6-0 at home in October, with Ian Rush scoring five to send the Reds top of the league. It was a position which Liverpool rarely slipped away from, with the only real challenge coming from Manchester United. A 4-0 loss at Coventry after going unbeaten for 15 games saw Fagan give his team a rollicking, but Liverpool consistently got the wins as United failed to take the initiative when the Reds dropped points.

A 0-0 draw away to Notts County secured Liverpool their 15th title as they became the first team since Arsenal to win three consecutive league championships. The Milk Cup had been won earlier as Fagan felt the relief of claiming his first trophy. Everton had been beaten 1-0 at Maine Road following a drab 0-0 draw at Wembley.

Europe, however, was where Liverpool looked especially impressive. Athletic Bilbao were beaten in a solid display after winning 1-0 away in the second leg, with the Basque side having only lost once in 31 European ties at home prior to being beaten by Liverpool. Benfica and Dinamo Bucharest were then dispatched to send Liverpool into a final against AS Roma in their intimidating Stadio Olimpico.

It was a stadium that brought back good memories for Liverpool as it was in Rome that the Reds won their first European Cup in 1977. They were in the Wolves' back yard and the Italians were favourites, boasting the likes of Bruno Conti and <u>Falcão</u>. It was in this cauldron of nostalgia, noise and nerves that Fagan found another level as he calmed and controlled his players before kick-off.

While Roma were placed in a training camp and kept to themselves, Liverpool went to Israel so the players could relax after a gruelling season. Despite Fagan's casual appearance, everything was meticulously planned. From toning down the training to building it up again, he was on top of everything. Fagan also ensured that Liverpool didn't arrive in Rome too early, so as to avoid boredom and over-thinking ahead of the final.

For Fagan it was about ensuring that the players were relaxed and feeling confident and ramping up the already intense pressure on Roma. He even delivered the UEFA instruction about players not running into the crowd if a goal was scored by saying "when *we* score a goal". It gave the players the belief that they could upset the Italians.

It had the required effect, with the players so relaxed that, after casually lapping up the atmosphere, they returned back to the tunnel and started to sing Chris Rea's song 'I Don't Know What It Is (But I Love It)', which became the unofficial song for the squad.

Nils Liedholm, the Roma manager, saw the colour on his players' face drain as they heard the Liverpool players in full voice. Although the Liverpool way was to let the opposition worry about them, Fagan still gave brief instructions that close tabs had to be kept on Falcão and Conti. However the main instruction was for Liverpool to play their natural game and enjoy the moment.

Phil Neal had given Liverpool the lead and, despite dominating the first half, Roberto Pruzzo had equalised for Roma just before the end of the half. No goals came in the second half or extra time, which meant that the European Cup final would be decided on penalties.

Whilst deciding who would take penalties, Fagan confidently told his players that he was proud of them and that all the pressure was now on Roma.

As Alan Kennedy scored the winning penalty for Liverpool, for Fagan it capped an unbelievable first season as Liverpool manager as they won a historic treble that no other English club had managed to do. Although Fagan had a beaming smile, his interviews were quietly understated as he also commiserated Roma on their defeat. His class always shone through.

The celebrations continued well into the night and there is an iconic picture of a relaxed Joe Fagan lounging casually in a deck chair by the pool with the European Cup as two Carabinieri stand guard. In many ways the image summed up Fagan. He might have given the air of a casual character but underneath there was solid determination to focus when he needed to.

Parties broke out across Liverpool as the Reds were welcomed home in an open bus tour. It was a welcome that the team and Joe Fagan thoroughly deserved, especially after many had questioned whether he had the skill to succeed Bob Paisley.

Anything after that magnificent season was always going to be an anti-climax and, with Souness going to Sampdoria, the task became trickier.

Jan Mølby and Paul Walsh had been signed but Liverpool got off to a terrible start to the season and at one point went seven games without a win. Fagan equally showed that there was no sentiment for players being picked purely on reputation as Kenny Dalglish was dropped for the first time away to Spurs. Although Liverpool lost 1-0 it showed that he had the ruthlessness to drop a big name. Contrary to what some people believe, Fagan, after two seasons in charge, had decided to step down at the end of the season prior to the final. The plan had been that Fagan would manage for two or three seasons with either Phil Neal or Kenny Dalglish to take charge after what he hoped would be a fitting finale.

Sadly that was not to be, with the horrific events of Heysel resulting in the deaths of 39 fans – mainly Juventus supporters. Despite the violence, the match was still played with Liverpool beaten after Michel Platini scored a penalty. However, the result had no real meaning.

The image of a broken Joe Fagan being supported by Roy Evans after Liverpool had touched down at Speke airport spoke volumes as to how it had affected him. It was something that he couldn't comprehend and was to force a sad end to an illustrious career. After all the years of loyal service to Liverpool, it should not be the lasting image of Joe Fagan nor should his achievements be forgotten, both as understudy to his more illustrious peers or during his lone stint in charge.

Joe Fagan, alongside Bill Shankly and Bob Paisley, did the most difficult thing in football by not just constantly adapting to the changes in the game but consistently staying one step ahead.

Paisley in his cardigan and Fagan in his flat cap may have looked and even acted like your favourite uncles but were as hard as nails if you was silly enough to cross them. They knew the ins and outs of the various personalities of footballers and as a result knew how to get the most out of them.

Playing under any of the three, you were expected to take personal responsibility and to give your all no matter what job you were given. Failure to do so would see you being shown the door. Reputations or egos didn't come into it. If you didn't do your job then you were no good to them.

That's not to say that it was ever easy. In many ways it may have been one of the reasons why Fagan had decided to step down as manager after two seasons. From reading the diary extracts of his authorised biography – by his son Andrew Fagan and Mark Platt – there appears to be a sense of frustration at not being able to work closely with his players in training. An extract from his second day as manager reads: "I have been here since 9.15am. The time now is 10.15am and there is no sign of anyone or anything happening. I am also dressed up in collar and tie. It is not my normal gear – but it becomes me."

Despite achieving unprecedented success in the short space of time that he was in charge of Liverpool, Fagan is largely forgotten outside of the club; not that it would have bothered him. He had no agendas and viewed football as simply doing a job. Indeed, he could never understand why people would still stop him in the street to chat about the game long after his retirement.

There is no doubt that Fagan was a down to earth man, with universal praise from the people he worked with. He was always as gracious in defeat as he was in victory, and would spend time with opposing managers – young and old – for the betterment of his own football knowledge and theirs.

While winning the treble in 1984 will undoubtedly go down as his premier achievement, his role in turning Liverpool from a struggling second tier club – alongside his great friends and peers, Shankly and Paisley – was both pioneering and undoubtedly vital.

His record stands above most managers and coaches to have ever been involved in professional football, and his personality separates him from so many of the brash, arrogant characters that have adorned our sport over the years. It's for these reasons that Joe Fagan deserves to be remembered as one of the finest coaches and managers in British football history.

THE SCOTCH PROFESSORS

Tactics in football are always constantly evolving. From the WM formation right through to the tika taka that has brought a lot of success to Barcelona and the Spanish national team respectively, coaches are always looking to stay one step ahead of their rivals.

Passing within football is seen as the main ingredient in the game. The question is devising a style that suits your team best and over the years there have been many debates as to which tactic brings the best chance of success. Whether it is the short passing and possession-based game or the Charles Reep long ball style it has generally been agreed that organisation and passing the ball is integral to football.

In the early days of association football this was not the case. Dribbling the ball as far as possible towards the opponent's goal and kicking the ball for someone to chase if they could get no further was how the game was played in its early years. This, it was deemed, was how football should be played as it displayed all the manly virtues of good honest pluck and endeavour.

Scotland was to shake this perception by introducing passing and in doing so invented the game that we know today. It was not done because it was aesthetically pleasing but to take advantage of the changes to the offside rule in 1867 which stated that a player was not offside providing that two opponents were between him and the goal.

This was a case of the Scots seeing an opportunity to use tactics to their advantage and was one of the major evolution changes in football as a result. Organisation and passing the ball to each other was seen as a far more effective and productive way of winning the game.

Queen's Park adopted this new style quite easily and probably had the better players at the time to implement this new approach. It also helped that the club was more enthusiastic and looking at ways at honing this new organised way of playing football rather than relying on a team of individuals trying to dribble towards goal.

Richard Robinson who wrote Queen's Park 150 year anniversary book stated that "Mondays, Wednesdays and Saturdays were fixed upon as the nights for play… Whoever selected the teams on practising nights had the power to place their men on the field, or appoint substitutes, and the players shall be bound to adhere to their instructions."

This new passing style of Queen's Park was already making people sit up and take notice. Many called it a "zig-zag," approach due to the way the ball was passed quickly between the Queen's Park team. In one match between Queen's Park and Wanderers the Glasgow Herald not only commented on the neat passing style but gave an in-depth description of the passing between the Queen's Park players.

More importantly for Queen's Park it was to bring much success to the club who dominated Scottish football between 1874 and 1893 as they won the Scottish Cup ten times within this period. They were also finalists twice in 1884 and 1885 in the FA Cup when Scottish teams were invited to enter the competition. Blackburn Rovers were the team who beat Queen's Park 2-1 and 2-0 respectively.

Although combination football, as it was called, was the adopted style amongst Scottish clubs it was to be an international match between Scotland and England in November 1872 that was meant to have caught the attention of the English who saw the benefits of a passing style.

Queen's Park made up the majority of the first eleven, but it wasn't just the familiarity between the players that persuaded the Scots to play a passing style. There was another tactical reason in the sense that they knew the English were bigger and stronger. If they tried to take on England at their game of dribbling and trying to use a physical approach, then there was a good chance that they would come out second best. Consequently, it was decided to adopt an organised passing style whereby they could control the game.

The game finished 0-0 but the Scottish passing style certainly drew attention from the English press. The London illustrated noted that "individual skill was generally on England's side but did not play to each other so well as their opponents, who seem to be adept in passing the ball."

Critics may have derided the Scottish way of playing the game as "unfootball like," but it showed that tactics in football were already being developed with Scotland being the leaders in the field.

It stood to reason that the Scottish influence of combination football would infiltrate the English game, with Jonathan Wilson in Inverting The Pyramid pointing to two Scotland internationals in particular – Henry Renny-Tailyour and John Blackburn. Both were lieutenants in the British army and played for the Royal Engineers who took the Scottish style to Kent. A former Sheffield United player, W.E. Clegg, noted how the change in tactics led to Sheffield United being beaten quite badly.

Others like the Reverend Spencer Walker, who had returned as a Master to Lancing College, saw the benefits of combination football or in his words "turning a mere bally-rag team into a well-ordered team." He delightedly noted the positive impact it had on his side after fixing positions for his players and instructing swift passing, and how it had baffled and bewildered their opponents. "They had a where do we come in look," he observed as Walker's team dominated proceedings.

The Scots' Professors

Although the benefits of passing were being noted, it was the rising professionalism of the English game that was to have more of an impact. With crowds and interest in football rising to huge heights, there were many ambitious clubs that wanted nothing but the best for their football team.

Scotland, therefore, was seen as fertile ground to recruit players who were not only noted for their ability, but also their tactical acumen. This, they felt, would increase their side's chances of success with the hope that the Scots in the team would pass on their knowledge to their English counterparts which earned them the nickname 'the Scotch Professors'. Advertisements were placed in Scottish newspapers that invited players to venture south and try out for a variety of clubs.

Many took up the opportunity with the likes of Scotland internationals Jimmy Douglas and Hugh McIntyre joining Blackburn Rovers with another James 'Reddie' Lang joining Wednesday. Of course, it was the financial incentive that led to many plying their trade in England which Lang duly noted years later when he admitted that he "had not gone down south to play for nothing."

There were many critics who lamented the way professionalism was creeping into football. Some even viewed Scottish players who took up the opportunity of playing in England as "traitorous wretches," with some even being blacklisted in representing the national side. This, though, was blowing against the wind as the ban was repealed in 1893 with Scottish clubs now allowed to become professional. Football, like its tactics, was now moving on to the next stage with combination football becoming the way to play.

Preston North End was the first club to benefit from recruiting the best players from north of the border and employing a more Scottish way of playing that brought them the success of their early years. The Glaswegian, James McDade, was signed for Preston and not only was he regarded as one of their best players, but influential on how they played the game as a team.

With a more organised structure, Preston was one step ahead of their rivals. In the 1888-89 inaugural season of the Football League, Preston not only went through the season unbeaten – sealing the nickname "The Invincibles" – but also won the FA Cup sealing the first ever double with another record of not conceding a goal. The league was retained the following year with Preston quickly becoming a dominant force in the English game.

Other clubs upon seeing the success of the Lancashire club continued to recruit Scottish players and adopt the tactics that was considered the norm in Scotland. Sunderland for instance had nine Scottish players (which included John Auld and Johnny Campbell, who was the top scorer in the league for three seasons in a row) helped Sunderland win three league titles.

In 1892, the newly formed Liverpool Football Club saw signing Scottish players as a way of quickly establishing themselves amongst the elite. So much so that after fielding an entire eleven in their first game against Rotherham they were nicknamed the "team of Macs."

Tom Watson – who had formerly managed Sunderland to their early league championship honours – was also responsible for Liverpool's first two First Division titles in 1900/01 and 1905/06 respectively. Part of his philosophy was to recruit players from Scotland as he felt that they could easily adapt to the combination football that he wanted his team to play as well as feeling that their ability was more than value for money.

The signing of the Scottish defender Alex Raisbeck from Stoke in 1898 demonstrated this train of thought – he was purchased not just for his ability as a player but his footballing brain. "His directors had every confidence in his judgement, and fearlessly relied on his opinion on all matters relating to the players and the matches of the moment." wrote the Liverpool Echo in 1924, fifteen years after he had left Liverpool.

There were, of course, complaints about the infiltration of Scottish players into the English game with the notable case of Upton Park who complained to the FA about the number of professional Scottish players within the line-up of their opposition, Preston North End. As a result, Preston were disqualified but this was more to do with the game becoming professional and the payments that were deemed to have been made. However, the incident inadvertently ensured that the game became recognised as professional when the following year such payments Preston had previously made were now legal.

The Scottish influence of how to play football was now becoming ingrained within the game as a whole. It had changed from the chaotic kicking game of early football matches to a more structured, organised game. Dribbling was still part of the game, but the team ethic now ruled. There was no more unruliness of eleven individuals running around and trying to dribble towards the opponent's goal.

It was inevitable in the next stage of combination football that teams expected their players to adopt positions to ensure that there was structure in their play. Most clubs now favoured a 2-3-5 formation but there were still critics who felt it was a disgrace that defenders now had a role in the game. The Scottish Athletic Journal spoke of "its disgust of certain country clubs keeping two players twenty yards from their own goal." However, with football clubs becoming successful using these tactics, it was another evolvutionary step to staying at the top.

Back then, as is the case now, coaches and players were always looking for the next advantage that would put them one step ahead of their rivals. So much so that the Arsenal centre-half Percy Sands in a 1907 article for the Sheffield Telegraph and Star Sports Special commented on whether "football was becoming more scientific?" In the piece he mused on the various thoughts and ideas of how football should be played. Whether it was the short passing game, the triangular movement, or the kick and rush style.

Tactics were discussed in the changing rooms prior to games with Tom Boyle, who captained both Burnley and Barnsley, commenting that the side with the best tactics will win the game. Any weaknesses in the opposition were to be exploited with players or play to be moved to that particular part of the field.

Scotland had led the way forward in making passing such an integral part of football as well as ensuring that there was organisation and a shape to the way they played the game.

As a result, combination football was the way to play with the 2-3-5 pyramid formation to be favoured for many years to come. There would be many variations of this system, most notably the Austrian Wunderteam, who played their centre forward in a more withdrawn system in the early 1930s which brought them success and credit.

Football tactics were constantly being assessed and scrutinised with the WM system introduced by Arsenal's Herbert Chapman being the next major change. That change, like the Scottish passing style, was through an amendment in the offside rule in 1925 that reduced the number of opposition players needed between themselves and the goal-line from three to two. Chapman used it to counter-attack the opposition quickly citing that the opposition was at its most vulnerable after losing possession. Arsenal were to benefit greatly from this tactic.

Tactics are constantly evolving from the push and run philosophy of Arthur Rowe's Tottenham to Barcelona and Spain's tiki taka. In the world of football, coaches are always looking to seek that extra edge whether through rule changes or simply using the players' and exploiting any weaknesses that they may see in the tactics used by the opposition. The English public schools may have introduced the 'modern' game to the world, but it was the Scots who started the 'big bang,' in terms of using tactics and believing that passing and organisation was far more effective than the mass brawl and disorganisation of early association football.

SOCRATES AND THE CORINTHIAN DEMOCRACY

With his beard, unkempt hair and stern look, there is an aura of a revolutionary about Sócrates. In some ways he was the footballing equivalent of Che Guevara, with his political opinions backed by his activism. To add weight to his mystique, Sócrates was one of the most elegant and gifted players to wear the yellow shirt of Brazil. He was also part of the 1982 and 1986 World Cup squads that played some of the most beautiful football ever seen at a major finals. With the likes of Falcão and Zico, it was a talented team that tore apart the opposition and scored spectacular goals like Sócrates' equaliser against the Soviet Union. All that seemed to matter to that Brazil teams of 1982 and '86 was the joy that they brought to people. They were Garrincha, just a few years later. Many Brazilians have fond memories of 'The Doctor', as he was nicknamed due to qualifying in medicine. Rumour had it that Socrates studied at University College Dublin but sadly was confirmed as an urban myth. He was seen as a leader of the people, who was kind and brought happiness with his football. Politics was also a passion of Sócrates, who had his eyes turned to the social injustices in his country. Brazil during the 1960s and '70s was a country ruled by a military junta following the 1964 Brazilian coup d'état, and culminated in the overthrow of the democratic João Goulart government. The previous regime was deemed to be a "socialist threat" by the military and the right-wing, who opposed policies such as the basic reform plan which was aimed at socialising the profits of large companies towards ensuring a better quality of life for Brazilians.

With the support of the US government, Goulart was usurped with Humberto de Alencar Castelo Branco sworn in as the president. Initially the aim of the junta was to keep hold of power until 1967, when Goulart's term would expire, but ultimately felt that they had to keep control to contain the "dissenters" within the country. Protests against the junta were brutally put down with dissenters killed, tortured or having to flee the country. Repression and elimination of any political opposition of the state became the policy of the government. The current Brazil president Dilma Rousseff was one of those who was imprisoned and tortured on the instructions of this totalitarian regime. The organisation and structure of football clubs were very much regimented, too – with little or no freedom to manoeuvre – which was in tune with the junta government. Players were expected to obey orders and were closely supervised; whether it was being told when they could eat or drink, or to having to be holed up in training camps days before matches. Initially, Sócrates along with his team-mates went along with this structure. However, he felt suffocated – famously a man of peace and freedom – and with the dictatorship strangling the life out of democracy in Brazil, believed that it was a time for change. Naturally, it was not something that Sócrates or his team-mates could openly discuss. Instead it had to be done subversively, behind the scenes and through the power of words. Many high-profile athletes in Brazil at the time were politically aware and felt that it was their duty to try to use sport to re-democratise Brazil and end the regime. An agreement was reached with the new club president Waldemar Pires in the early-1980s which allowed Sócrates and his team-mates to have full control of the team and to establish a democratic running of the club. During a meeting in which everyone got an opportunity to speak freely, it was agreed that every decision would be decided by the collective. This would be when the squad would train, eat or, as Waldemar expressed in a documentary about the Corinthians team, "when they would stop on the coach for a toilet break". What made the Corinthians democracy even more unique was that voting wasn't restricted to the playing and coaching staff; it was a model that involved everyone within the club. Whether it was the players, masseurs, coaches or cleaners, everybody had a say. In short it was 'one person, one vote' with everyone backing the majority verdict. After agreeing the new structure it was first put to the test when Corinthians went on tour in Japan. Walter Gasagrande, who was 19 at the time, was heavily in love and wanted to fly back home to his girlfriend. A vote was called for with people speaking for and against Gasagrande being able to return to Brazil. It was decided that he would have to stay – and Gasagrande respected the decision. Nothing was off-limits at discussions with it being agreed that a psychiatrist was to be hired in order to help the team. Sócrates and his colleagues had an open mind and invited people who interested them outside of football. Prominent artists, singers, and filmmakers were invited to speak on various topics.

Corinthians slowly embodied the dream of the ordinary Brazilian in removing the dictatorship, to be replaced with universal suffrage. This was markedly expressed on the back of the club shirt which had 'Corinthians Democracy' printed with splashes of mock red blood similar to the Coca-Cola logo. It was a move that upset the prominent right-wing, many of whom had branded the Corinthians' Democracy movement as "anarchists" and "bearded communists". However, with football coming to represent the very essence of Brazil even the junta government knew that they had to tread carefully. Nonetheless, the government still warned them about interfering in politics. Indeed, they had used the success of the 1970 World Cup for their own devices, so much so that Sócrates stated: "Our players of the 1960s and 1970s were romantic with the ball at their feet, but away from the field absolutely silent. Imagine if at the time of the political coup in Brazil a single player like Pele had spoken out against all the excesses." Sócrates and his team-mates were prepared to bring in a silent revolution by using football to speak out against the military junta. The first multiparty elections since 1964 were set for the May provincial elections in 1982. Despite this, the majority of Brazilians were scared of voting. Some didn't even know whether the army would allow them to vote, while others thought it safer not to vote at all. With the May provincial elections set for the 15, the Corinthians team decided to up the ante and to chip away at the dictatorship. They agreed that they would have 'on the 15th, vote' on the back of their shirts to encourage people to head to the polls. It was a quiet voice of dissent but as a smiling Sócrates advises in an interview years later, the military junta could hardly object as the team was not backing any particular party, merely encouraging people to vote. Corinthians' mood was quickly picked up by Brazilians, with the military government taking a battering in the provincial elections. It now appeared that the regime was losing its grip on power. Sócrates later said: "[It was the] greatest team I ever played in because it was more than sport. My political victories are more important than my victories as a professional player. A match finishes in 90 minutes, but life goes on." With the thirst for democracy at its peak, Corinthians now pushed for presidential elections. The team now took to the field with 'win or lose, always with democracy' emblazoned on their jersey this time. It was a mood that was quickly engulfing the ordinary Brazilian, who sensed that they could push for democracy.

During this period the Timão won the 1982 and 1983 São Paulo Championship. Unsurprisingly, considering his talent, Sócrates was highly sought after by top European clubs. In 1984, he proclaimed at a large rally that if congress passed through the amendment for free presidential elections then he would stay in Brazil. A huge cheer went up but sadly the amendment fell and Sócrates moved to Fiorentina. Brazilians, in the words of Sócrates, were beginning to realise that political change was possible. It was something that the military government couldn't stop, and so it was in 1985 that they were defeated in the presidential elections. Finally, Corinthians had achieved their objective of returning democracy back to Brazil. It was a dream that Sócrates and the club were proud of bringing to the fore.

By using football, they had managed to get their message across and helped bring about the change that people wanted. In many ways, it is quite fitting that since football is in the bloodline of Brazil, it was the Sócrates and the Corinthians Democracy that was part of the movement that helped rid the nation of the military government. A first class player and man, there are few footballers with the same skill and integrity of the great Doctor Sócrates. It is why, after passing away in 2011, that he was revered with a fitting tribute by Corinthians players and supporters who held their fist out in memory of their legendary brother.

BIBLIOGRAPHY

Towers, Brian, 'The rise and fall of Liverpool's dockland, Waterfront blues,' Carnegie publishing limited, 2011

Taplin, Eric, 'Near to revolution: the Liverpool general transport strike of 1911,' The Bluecoat Press; 1st edition, November 1994

Craig, Maggie, 'When the Clyde ran red, A social history of Clydeside, Birlinn books, 2011

Hattersley, Roy, 'The Great Outsider, David Lloyd George,' Abacus, 2012

Mann, Tom, 'The memoirs of Tom Mann,' Forgotten books, 2018

Renwick, Chris, 'Bread for all. The origins of the welfare state,' Penguin books, 2017

Smith, Harry Leslie, 'Harry's Last Stand,' Icon books, 2014

Toye, Richard, 'Lloyd George & Churchill. Rivals for greatness' Macmillan books, 2007

Webb, Simon, '1919 Britain's year of revolution,' Pen and sword books ltd, 2016

Welch, Ellen, 'The NHS at 70. A living history,' Pen and sword books ltd, 2018

The Liverpool General Transport Strike 1911; reprinted from the transactions of the Historic Society of Lancashire and Cheshire, volume 13, pages 169-195

Newspaper sources

Daily Courier, 29th June 1911

Liverpool Daily Post and Mercury, 15th August 1911, 21st, 22nd 25th August 1911

Liverpool Echo, 14th August 1911, 18th August 1911

Liverpool Daily Post. Liverpool strike-ridden: 15,000 men revolt; abridged extract from a contemporary newspaper account of the railwaymen's strike, page 74, 1955

Liverpool Post and Mercury, 7th, 11th, 19th June 1919

Liverpool Courier, 11th June

Liverpool Weekly Post 14th, 21st June

Online sources

Royden, Mike 'The Liverpool Transport Strike, 1911,' www.roydenhistory.co.uk

www.oldpolicecellsmuseum.org.uk/content/history/police_history_strike_19 18-1919

www.nationalarchives.gov.uk/cabinetpapers/alevelstudies/origins-nhs.htm

The start of the NHS, www.nhshistory.net/shorthistor.htm

1945-51: Labour and the creation of the welfare state, www.theguardian.com/politics/2001/mar/14/past.education

BBC – History – World Wars: Why Churchill lost in 1945, www.bbc.co.uk/history/worldwars/wwtwo/election_01

1911: Liverpool General Transport Strike, www.libcom.org/history/1911-Liverpool-general-transport-strike

Lamb, Dave, The Southampton mutiny, www.libcom.org/history/articles/southampton-mutiny-1919

The Calais mutiny, www.libcom.org/history/articles/calais-mutiny

Sources for football articles

Wilson, Jonathan, The football pyramid, Orion books limited, 2008

Fagan, Andrew, Platt, Mark, 'Joe Fagan. The reluctant Champion,' Aurum press limited, 2011

Tompkins, Paul, 'Dynasty. Fifty years of Shankly's Liverpool,' GPRF publishing, 2008

ABOUT THE AUTHOR

Brian Benjamin is an author from Liverpool. When he isn't out and about walking with Fudge the dog, Brian tries to spend time writing. He has previously contributed a variety of articles For These Football Times website.

You can read more of Brian's articles on his blog Graffiti at chbenj23.wordpress.com

It's a shame about Matt was self-published in 2013 and The Terry Lamont story in 2016.

Printed in Great Britain
by Amazon

51062711R00078